Compassionism

Helping Business Leaders
Create Engaged Teams
and Happy People

Kavitha Chahel

Compassionism

First published in 2016 by

Panoma Press Ltd
48 St Vincent Drive, St Albans, Herts, AL1 5SJ, UK

info@panomapress.com
www.panomapress.com

Book design and layout by Neil Coe.
Illustrations by Roger Penwill.

Printed on acid-free paper from managed forests.

ISBN 978-1-784520-94-6

The right of Kavitha Chahel to be identified as the author of this work has been asserted in accordance with sections 77 and 78 of the Copyright, Designs and Patents Act 1988.

A CIP catalogue record for this book is available from the British Library.

This book is available online and in bookstores.

Dedications

To my husband, for being my rock and soul mate.

To my mother, for showing me that the most important thing in this world is compassion.

To my papa, for teaching me the value of hard work and perseverance.

To my brother, for always finding unique ways of pushing me to be better.

CONTENTS

"They always say time changes things, but you actually have to change them yourself."

Andy Warhol

Acknowledgements

Many thanks to my wonderful husband Markand, for being my gravity and helping me stay focused and sticking with it, I have learnt so much about love and connectedness from being with you. You are my lighthouse and I am blessed to have you in my life.

To my brother Miki, for sharing life with me, you have been more like a father than a brother, thank you for always nudging me to be a better version of myself and being so protective of me. I would not have been able to achieve any of what I have done without your support.

To my parents Biba and Kuldeep, you respected my individuality and independence. You let me fly and have always been there to catch me. To my mother, with whom I have had so many adventures, whose generosity of spirit, drive, passion and compassion shaped my life. Mum, you are always proud of me and believe in me, even when I didn't believe in myself. Thank you for every single sacrifice you made for me. To my father, whose amazing medical mind taught me to be curious and question the 'rules' and to be a nonconformist, to live my life my own way, thank you for teaching me to be tough and being the voice of reason and practicality. To my beautiful grandmothers whose stories, love and protection will stay with me forever.

Thank you to my in-laws, Jaymin and Jayshee for your acceptance and love.

To my godparents Denise and Terry, I am humbled by your kindness, generosity and love.

To my nieces and nephews, the next generation of leaders, it is you who inspire me to want to offer the solution of compassionate communication to 'heal' and solve the issues in the workplace.

To all my friends, you are my support and source of much laughter. Thank you for being there for me and always believing in me. I have nothing but love for you. I would also like to thank all of my extended family and family friends for being absolute angels and cheeky little devils. You give me love, laughter, adventure and great stories. Without you all my life would be a lot less interesting. I love you and am grateful you are in my life. And I thank all the people who've come into my life and enriched it in some way. I would name all of you but that would take up another book in itself.

I would like to extend my gratitude to the following individuals for helping me shape my business. You offered me advice and a forum for networking. To Jenny, my incredible brand consultant, for her belief in me and kindly writing me a review. My dear friend Carole, who generously shared her wonderful stories of her adventures in Africa with me, which I have used in the book. Sarah and Kevin, who have set up the 30-day blogging challenge, you gave me a forum for sharing my blog posts on compassionate communication. To Tim, thank you for designing my very first official business logo. To everyone at Panoma Press, Mindy, Emma, Alison and Neil, the designer, thank you for your support. To Roger Penwill for the book illustrations. Thanks to everyone who helped and supported my writing and work.

To all the teachers I have ever had in my life, thank you for sharing your knowledge and infinite energy. Thank you, Justin who generously wrote the foreword for this book, whose testimonial has been used on the cover. Thank you, Chiara and Carlos for taking time out of your very busy schedules and agreeing to review the book for me. Also a big thank you to all the people who let me have an insight into their workplace by hiring me as an employee or coach. Thanks for all the experiences, the good the bad and the ugly.

I would also like to say a very special thank you to all the people below who subscribed to my YouTube channel, to enable me to get a customised URL in time for the publication of the book. Now you can find www.youtube.com/compassionismltdkc on there with ease. In no particular order:

Markand Patel, Mandeep Chahel, Conchitta Afser, Kiron Chahel, Fiona Watson, Pawan Bhullar, Keshy Dhillon, Akash Patel, Krupa Patel, Johnny Omar, Chris Halicki, Eveline Ali-Khan, Adam Ali-Khan, Fia Tarrant Ali-Khan, Jamil Ali-Khan, Rumi Agarwal, Claire Sidebottom, Sara Wonderland, Jenny Andersson, Maggie Moog, Karuna Pillai, Anthony Dinesh Michael, Anoushka HG, Shahee Warner, Soraya Louisa Putra, Faryal Azlin, Abel Ataelsaid, Richie-Rich & Kris, Liew Tze-Ern, Rob Sheffield, Averil Mullarkey, Fanoula Grekos, Oscar Tindall, Carole Chapman, Inka Wibowo, Chris Torruella, Evan Day, Julianne Muli, Natasha Rose, Gaby Gabriela, Carly Jenner, Jack Yallop, Jigna Patel, Rehan Gomez, Celine 'possum' Bilham, Tina Kramer Jen, Alison Sauter Bock, Adele Simor, Jenn-Hui Tan, Divyesh Patel, Rebecca & Alain Partridge, Ellie Burgess, Lawrence Broom, Umang Patel, Vilasini Theva, Nim Thiagarajah,

Carina D'Souza, Camila S.L. Miranda, Lalit Sethi, James Grant, Geoff Rea, David Dingvean, Sahil Sodhi, Hiromi Stone, Baldeep Bhullar, Nicola Mullarkey, Cindy Gan, Glen Savage, Connor Martin, Gene Hewitt, Grant Telfer, Gregory Baker, Deeya Menon, Yilan Lee, Veronique Schnoering, Deepa Mireless, Jan Dryden, Lizzie Nolan, Laura Liles, Anita Js Bassette, Philip Chadha, Rory Reid, Sarah Arrow (and everyone associated with the 30 blogging challenge who also subscribed), Neha Mistry, Amanda Clarke, Lyndsey Owen, Soraya Ramana, Beckett 'Bexiita Pole', Simon Rodd, Sherry Bevan, Lisa Williams, Harpreet Chahal, Harry Patel, Danielle O'Driscoll, Irene Yoo, Lina Wheeler, Jemma Oval, Lucy Reed, Briony Hovarth, Brenda Boateng, Jay Diamond, Mindy Gibbins-Klein, Jessica Boylen, Anoja Neill, Lucy Wilson, Karen McManus, Gurjit Sidhu and to anyone who I may have accidentally left out, you know who you are, thank you for helping me!

If I have forgotten to mention you and you subscribed, please accept my sincere apologies. Do let me know and I promise to make it up to you somehow.

Foreword

Compassion in the workplace isn't just some hippy notion of employee togetherness. Encouraging compassion, mindfulness, respect, acceptance and healthier, more human relationships can help companies grow, improve innovation and ultimately improve profits.

In today's world, work practices are changing: the rise of the virtual worker, the importance of innovation and adaptability. Today's worker is looking for more than just a decent pay cheque, bonus and dental insurance. A sense of belonging, being part of something bigger than yourself, working with organisations and colleagues that have the right outlooks, attitudes and values. It means having a sense of purpose – being excited to go to work every day and not dreading it. It means giving 110% rather than clock-watching for 5.30pm.

With professional networking sites (such as Glassdoor and LinkedIn), employees can turn the spotlight on their employers, their innermost workings and tell the world how the company really operates. At best it becomes a forum to share your pride and advocacy for your co-workers, at worst a platform to expose intercompany feuds, high staff churn, a toxic environment of bullying, bureaucracy and inequality.

If left unchecked this can do untold damage to your brand and your ability to hire the top talent needed to grow.

In Compassionism, Kavitha explores the tell-tale signs of this toxic environment, the impact it has on business and explores concepts, ideas and practical steps you can take to improve your own company's outlook on mindfulness in the workplace.

Justin Hall, CEO of Protocol Global Ltd.

Preface

The vision that motivates me is for us to all live in a world in which people communicate with compassion. My mission is to help people connect deeply with an awareness of self, their infinite inner resources and resilience to really listen and communicate from a place of balance and create really exciting new options for co-creating and being generative.

I define compassionate communication as a way of communicating while remaining connected to your humanity and to the other person's humanity, even when there is a difficult message or emotion that needs to be expressed. It is not all about being 'fluffy' or 'lovey-dovey', it is an honest, open and deeply connected way of communicating and requires you to learn to be comfortable with your vulnerability.

Having worked in the wildly different public health, charity and corporate sectors, the one thing I have found is that the majority of work environments are fairly toxic. It is the general lack of respect, not seeing value in one another and dehumanisation of the workforce which causes a great deal of stress and angst, and a vicious cycle is created. In this book I have shared stories from my own experiences as an employee and a coach, not to humiliate or shame anyone but to use as examples of how not to do something. Sometimes, without even realising, you can self-sabotage your own business and be your own worst enemy.

No one is perfect, and we are all filled with flaws but we all have our strengths. We can all learn to communicate with compassion and help create teams that are:

- Effective

- Efficient

- Productive

The new way of communicating will help decrease misunderstandings and create a new way of solving problems, which will ultimately lead to more:

- Wealth being generated

- A happier working environment

Taking the necessary action to get to know yourself and manage your own stress allows you the head space to give time and energy to other people when you speak with them. To really connect to your compassion and in turn create a culture and work environment where employees want to make a positive contribution.

Not all business leaders/department heads have good people skills or even know how they come across to others. The way we communicate or don't communicate can create conflict and cause us to not trust one another. Improving the way in which we communicate and lead naturally enriches how you relate to people in relationship with them, improves your support network and will ultimately change your business from surviving to thriving. This book will show you how to add more value to others whilst gaining more for yourself. Everyone wants to succeed at something; give people the opportunity to rise to the occasion and you may just be surprised by the level of loyalty and the creativity they are willing to share.

We live in a volatile world and we are called as individuals to make a difference; the way we can do this is by doing so collectively. To create a way of being that brings compassion to every interaction into the wider community and world, not just for improving our business. I believe that the people who wish to become compassionate leaders and are taking all the necessary actions to learn to communicate with compassion are part of creating a better world for us all to be a part of, be it with your family, your business, your teams or your community.

Thank you for reading and sharing this book and putting into action what you learn.

My warmest and best wishes to you.

Kavitha Chahel

Introduction

Being a leader is a fairly thankless role; if things go wrong you are responsible and if things go right you feel guilty for taking the credit for someone else's hard work. Taking on this role feels like walking around with a bull's eye stuck to your back, which can manifest into feelings of isolation and loneliness, and so therein begins the development of unhealthy and unhelpful behaviour patterns to deal with the demands of the role. When you feel isolated the last thing you instinctively want to do is show any weakness. In the act of being strong you end up coming across as being cold and detached, to try and hide any weakness. Dealing with a crowded and competitive marketplace also causes leaders to develop certain behaviour patterns that are not conducive to being an effective leader.

There is no shame in admitting that someone else may be more knowledgeable than you, yet you would rather shout than admit you are wrong. Trying to live up to what everyone expects of you, ignoring advice or assistance because they are admissions of your shortcomings, is a recipe for disaster.

The way in which you deliver a message and what you say can either make or break your business. Create a business environment that people want to be a part of and in doing so, significantly increase your profits, simply by making humanity a priority. This book is for you, the business leaders, who in an ever saturated and competitive market want to increase their profits and overcome the growth 'slump', to move from a business that merely exists to one that is really thriving. Discover how being a more self-aware leader and communicating with compassion will help you.

The book is packed with practical tips, exercises and simple strategies of:

- **S**elf-awareness

- **A**cceptance

- **M**indfulness

- **E**ngagement

The way people communicate with one another at work is a problem that, quite frankly, has a very simple sustainable solution. The manner in which we communicate with others at work, be they colleagues or clients, can have a significant impact on the outcome of a situation. On the one hand, when proper care and consideration is not taken, the way in which we communicate can add significant levels of stress to your life and that of your employees. On the other hand, when well-informed and honest communication is achieved, that interaction can be generative and help create something new out of what was once a difficult situation. In doing so, more options and possibilities become available to us than previously.

We've all been a part of and contributed to a society where profits have become more important than humanity. My role is to help business leaders to become part of the solution to these problems alongside making a profit. What if you were told that the way you or your employees communicated contributed to creating an unpleasant, at worst 'toxic' work environment and this impacted your profits? Would you then be willing to put in the necessary effort to make the changes and create an environment that encouraged compassion, and by doing so increase your profit? Thereby creating a workforce that was more productive, creative and collaborative? I am certain the answer would be yes. It amazes me that there are so few organisations that are willing to spend money, time or effort in doing this. Instead, the solutions that are put in place to 'fix' these problems and increase team cohesion are at best superficial and at worst patronising. Research commissioned by the O.C.Tanner Company and conducted by noted research firm The Jackson Organization of Columbia, Maryland, found that companies that effectively appreciate employee value enjoyed a return on equity and assets between 2.4% to 8.7% more than experienced by firms that don't.

It is very easy to simply blame external economic factors, your competitors and staff for your organisation not doing well and desperately scramble to create new product offerings as a remedy. Often the real solution is at the end of your nose and you just have not seen it. Business leaders can unintentionally hinder the business and the people within the business from truly reaching their full potential and from overcoming their hurdles to growth. One of the ways they do this is by either contributing to or allowing people to speak to each other badly, thus adding stress to people who are already stressed from the targets they have to achieve and customers they need to keep happy.

Toxic work environments lead to high staff turnover and only 7% of organisations actually calculate the cost of staff turnover to their organisation *(CIPD survey: Recruitment, retention and turnover, 2004).* The majority of people surveyed agreed that turnover has a negative effect on organisation performance. This is as true today as it was 12 years ago when the survey was conducted. Do you know the cost to you and your organisation when someone leaves? Well apparently the average cost of replacing a senior employee is about £8,000 (US$11,280) and £5,000 (US$7,050) for a mid-level employee, which does not take into account the months it will take you to get the new employee ramped up to working at full capacity.

We have as much a capacity for love as we do for hatred. As much as we demand the truth, we often do not like to hear it. The truth forces us to address issues we are often ill-equipped to deal with, and it's often easier to just ignore situations in the hope that they go away. In the meantime we carry on doing what we have always done, not because we are stupid enough to believe that we will get different results by doing the same thing over and over, it's just that it's easier to do what we have always done, and it is the only way we know. Some of us have no intention or desire to do anything differently. We are all one big contradiction; we are as kind as we are cruel. This cruelty, if one is not a sociopath, is usually driven by fear. Fear of losing out on something or the fear of change. I have also seen cruelty driven by the need to preserve the status quo.

I was once a whistleblower who raised the issue of bullying in the workplace with the HR department, with details of all the bullying that was going on in the department with people in the team. What I learnt was that this truth just caused the heads of the organisation to panic. The best solution would have been for HR to address the issues with the person concerned and the company to invest in coaching for everyone involved, to try and uncover the root of the matter and help people learn to communicate effectively. Speak your truth but in a way that you stay grounded and connected within yourself, with empathy for the other person.

It is seen as easier by business leaders to just pay employees off with severance packages or to put people through performance reviews in the hope that they will leave themselves once they get stressed enough. Instead of dealing with the real problem, the solution seems to be to raise the stress levels. No organisation wants to be taken to tribunal for bullying/discrimination/unfair dismissal. It doesn't look good for them and no employee really wants to take the employer to tribunal as it only adds to an already stressful situation. There is a better way.

It was my experience as an employee (the other side of the fence) that really got me started on this journey of how to help people learn to communicate with compassion. Spending the next few years learning, observing and looking for solutions to the very problems I had seen unfold in front of me. To be the kind of business leader you wish you could have, one that is empathetic, helps others succeed, empowers them, celebrating each of the successes they have had and coaching them through their communication issues.

Don't be too hard on yourself. No one gets given a road map when they become a business leader. The reality of most business training that is available is that no one really attends more than a day or two of people-management training. I have been on a few people-management training courses and shockingly more time is spent at these training sessions with other attendees having a moan about the people on their teams. Moaning about how to dismiss someone that you no longer want in your team, the dreaded performance review or putting someone back on probation or extending their probation. The focus is often on all the legal ways you can remove staff. Your time and energy is best spent on awareness training; to be aware of self and aware of the other as a human. More emphasis needs to be placed on learning how to communicate with compassion.

If someone in your team is consistently underperforming and you've invested the time and effort to help them work out the root cause of the issues and provided the necessary support to help them, and there is no change or improvement, then it is completely understandable that you will want them gone. Employees need to be engaged, proactive and working efficiently. It's OK for people to have the occasional 'off day' or even the 'off week' where there is perhaps a dip in performance. But if it becomes a habit, no employer should have to put up with it, especially if there has been every effort made to help.

I implore you, be it in your personal life or your work life, if there is something under the surface that needs addressing do not just react to the symptoms and throw someone under a bus, address the real issues. You will not uncover what those issues are by shouting at someone or pleading with them. If you don't know how to do it yourself, then get a coach or a business therapist. They are trained to help and facilitate in addressing the issues. Do you want a great business management team? Then learn and teach them how to accept joint responsibility with their teams, by communicating with them in a way that is generative and brings out the best in people.

Imagine, if you will, an office of people, now imagine that these employees feel they have the best boss they have ever worked with, one who speaks to them with respect, even when there is a difficult message to deliver. A boss who empowers them to make decisions and teaches them how to be responsible for their actions. A boss who takes the time to understand what went wrong and takes overall responsibility. Someone who is happy to brainstorm and train when needed. The type of boss who is happy to coach or invest in coaching, to help people learn how to communicate more effectively. Everyone actually enjoys coming into work each day and knows if they have to leave early for whatever reason or come in late that their boss will understand, so long as they complete their tasks or objectives, or put in the additional work when it's needed.

Now try and picture the opposite of that, it's tricky right? It's not a very nice experience to picture people miserable, rude and unhappy. Toxic environments in the work place lead to you not making the profits that you potentially could, staff not getting the pay rise and bonuses they are hankering for and no one wins.

From 2000 I have invested a lot of my time and finances in studying human psychology and learning therapeutic techniques that can be used in the business world. Since 2009, I've applied this learning with business leaders in coaching and training to help them bring more compassion to the world, starting with the way we communicate with one another and ultimately to make more money – a no-brainer really. Going through the book chapter by chapter with an open heart and open mind, do as many of the exercises as you can as you go along. Use the appropriate exercises with your team when you see the opportunity to do so. You can either scribble directly in the book, or get a notebook to use that you can keep and refer back to.

I've included illustrative stories, to inspire you to do something differently, or try something new. So as not to divulge people's personal details, all the names I have used have been changed.

Bring more humanity and empathy to your encounters with everyone whom you work with and create meaningful connections. I hope you thoroughly enjoy the transformation that more compassion will bring to your business.

Chapter 1:
The truth about the hurdles and the struggle zones

The struggle zones of a growing organisation are largely down to the way in which we communicate or don't communicate. The way people speak to one another in business is often appalling. How can your business grow and thrive if the environment you have helped create is in fact toxic? When ex-employees or disgruntled customers write poor reviews of your business, just know that prospective customers and employees may very well see these reviews. It is also not that uncommon for SME's to be heavily reliant on one customer for the majority of their income. It is a risk to do this and the need should be to expand the customer base. In doing this, remember your reputation is everything so keep your eye on the ball and get your heart involved in your business.

In order to bring more compassion into your business, it is important to identify what and where your organisation's struggle zones are. Only then can you embark on working out what can be done about them. It is likely that you have some awareness of what these issues might be and the departments struggling the most. Just to be certain, a business consultant can really come in handy in running an unbiased audit, to help you identify the problem areas and work with you on a plan of action to fix them.

The pressure cooker

The pressure cooker situation is one everyone in the work environment will be able to relate to. It is a very common issue when you work with clients/customers, have account managers/customer service teams who look after them, and very often there are suppliers/third party agencies thrown into the mix as well. There may be a few internal teams that need to work together to deliver on a particular job or project.

This involves the boss, the rest of the leadership team, sales and operations, occasionally there are external parties thrown in for good measure, with all the different personalities and expectations, goals and agendas. The heat that is put underneath them all in the form of poor communication, demands, time constraints and a lack of expectation management in turn creates a huge amount of pressure. The outcome of this is the 'steam' which is the misunderstandings, annoyance, anger, stress, dissatisfaction, burnout etc.

Pressure cooker situations are a by-product of a lack of communication and expectation management. There are two main types of pressure cooker environments: the internal pressure cooker and the external pressure cooker. The external pressure cooker is not entirely external; it is a combination of the internal pressure cooker with the addition of external demands and third party agency issues.

The internal pressure cooker

You have to deliver results on projects and meet deadlines to make money, and you have to also keep your promises to your clients. Some stress is perfectly normal and expected at work, it is what keeps us going. When people are under excessive levels of stress, one of the side effects is the worst parts of our egos rear their ugly heads and colleagues lash out at one another, layering on even more stress and making unrealistic demands of each other's time. Often in a pressure cooker situation there is a sales person involved, someone from operations and the boss.

The sales person

The sales person thinks their demands should be met and their ideas are the best. They don't seem to understand that there may be problems with meeting the demands and why individuals in the other departments are making such a fuss. From the perspective of the sales person, operations should just be grateful that a project has been sold; after all, it's the sales person that brings in the business that enables everyone to get wages, so there is a general feeling that operations should just be grateful. The time frames that I as the sales person agreed with the client are what they are, so everyone should just get on with it.

The operations person

The operations person gets frustrated with the sales team: "*Bloody sales, what do they know about scheduling and what is involved in getting things delivered on time? They are too busy sat in the pub drinking beers at the end of each quarter, from midday, while I am slogging my guts out trying to get things finished so they can get their damn commission cheque at the end of it all. It is not fair, sales get to go out on client jollies while I have to sit here and fix the mess their unrealistic demands create.*" The boss just wants work to get done, make money and for the clients not to complain.

The boss

The boss knows that the sales team all have an ego that is difficult to manage. Sales brings in money and hits their targets, so bosses will continue to turn a blind eye to their attitude. The boss knows that operations will complain. There is generally an attitude of, *"They will always find something to complain and moan about. There is too much work or there is too little work. They do always manage to get work done to tight deadlines. Why can't they all just learn to play nice? And let me get on with fronting our brand and making new connections."*

Such pressure cooker situations create stressful disharmonious ego-driven environments, which add unnecessary stress. It drives further division between people with already different personalities, work ethics and styles.

This division and pressure cooker situation occurs within teams where each person believes their own perspective is the right one and each individual knows best. There is a need for leaders to learn how to facilitate compassionate communication within teams, by learning to communicate with compassion. Moving past the 'he said/she said' hurdle can be challenging.

The external pressure cooker

The external pressure cooker is a little trickier to navigate through. The big personalities and ego clashes of the internal pressure cooker is certainly no walk in the park. In the situation of the external pressure cooker environment, you are often held over a barrel with your pants around your ankles because you are trying to please your clients and meet their demands. The external pressure cooker is an amalgamation of the internal pressure cooker and external stakeholders (be it the client/supplier or another third party). Unless you, as the business leader, step in to set up the boundaries or step back and allow your team to set the boundaries, the heat gets turned up under everyone.

The external pressure cooker has the issues of poor communication, demands, time constraints and a lack of expectation management that cause the pressure to rise, only this time there are even more people in the mix, over and above those in the internal pressure cooker. It is important to keep clients happy; after all, it is the business from them that helps you pay staff, your bills, and your own salary. Clients also bring with them the brand names, which let you show off your latest and greatest conquests. The question is at what cost will you keep clients happy? You need to know where the boundary lines of doing business together are, which have to be communicated.

There are some boundaries that are hard boundaries, those which you will not move for anything, such as not tolerating aggressive behaviour. Other boundaries (soft boundaries) can have some flexibility to them, for example: I do not take client calls over the weekend, because I value my time with my family and friends. If, however, for some reason there is an urgent project that needs delivering then I will adjust this boundary accordingly. The movement of a soft boundary should only be done as the exception and not become the norm. You have to communicate your boundaries to your clients and they need to know how far they can push for delivery. This creates a respectful working partnership that works for everyone involved.

The suppliers, like clients, have their own internal politics and dramas to deal with; third party companies often don't want to work with you, sometimes due to some kind of rivalry, and partners are often too far removed from the ethos and values of your organisation and make huge demands on your time. All of this adds to the mounting tension within the pressure cooker.

The simple truth is that businesses exist to make money. You are a business leader, with a want to take over the world and be the best. This desire for world domination and drive to be the best puts a great deal of stress on employees. Ambition is healthy and it is good to keep challenging yourself to be better and work that little bit harder. After all, we all like value for money, but I have seen this play out negatively time and time again; the client puts pressure on you and you in turn put pressure on your staff. The staff 'break their balls' trying to get things done just as you want, and it becomes a vicious cycle, ending up with a build-up of tension and ill will, from a lack of empathy and communication. Clients are, within their organisations, under pressure to perform and produce results. They have to prove their worth in an environment which may feel like a political minefield.

I am very often heard saying, "Start as you mean to go on". It helps manage expectations and allows you to communicate with compassion. I recall having a conversation with a gentleman who interviewed me, whom I ended up working with for many years. The conversation went along these lines: I let him know I was very dedicated, would work hard and deliver results. I also added that I would not check my work emails after 7pm or over the weekends regularly. I let him know I would check my emails when I came into the office in the morning, so not to expect a response from me in the middle of the night. I did so every so often, on the occasional few days every few months that were very busy and I would have to work late. I started as I meant to go on. My clients knew not to expect me to reply to messages at night, and my boss understood. They also knew that when there was something that needed my attention I would give it 100%. If there was a proposal due, or if my operations team needed me to be around late, I would be in the office till the cleaners had been and gone (you know when it gets a little scary when the only light left on in the office is the one above your head).

Expectation management is about communicating the boundaries and what is possible within specific time frames. A big NO in good business is overpromising, never overpromise and under deliver. It is far better to be realistic about what you can achieve within the given time and resources that you have available to you. If things go wrong, which they do on occasion, it must be communicated and expectations need to be adjusted accordingly. If you do not communicate to your clients/suppliers, the risk is the loss of business and your reputation. If a project is going really well, communicate that too. Communicating and being transparent sets the scene, it lets people know the boundaries. I remember saying to a team whom I had not long worked with that I wanted the long hours they worked to be the exception and not the norm. The message that regularly working outside your contracted hours sends is that you are allowing clients to flag everything as critical or urgent. Manage your employees' time and manage people's expectations of you. People may not like the boundary you put up, but will respect the boundaries and you for it. It also reduces the heat under the pressure cooker, so the top gets blown less often.

My team remind me often of what I had said to them in one of our weekly meetings. I did not want to regularly get emails from them at 11.30pm. At that time of night I expected them to be doing one of the following things: out with their friends, asleep, having sex, watching a movie, cuddling with their children/partner, having a relaxing bath, or doing something else they enjoyed. I did not want them sending messages at a time they needed to use to unwind and de-stress. Yes, we are all adults, but your employees will sometimes do things just to impress you or just simply take on too much because they feel that unless they do that they will never progress. Seriously, there is no such thing as a work/life balance, it is all life. As a business leader if you learn to set boundaries of your own and encourage your staff to do the same for themselves, you can reduce the pain of the pressure cooker environment.

Change brings growth

Another struggle zone a business faces is when its organic growth seems unable to surmount the £4m hurdle (US$6m). The current growth trajectory you have for the last few years reaches a plateau and things have begun to stagnate. Businesses typically start off relatively small, either a few people around a kitchen table or huddled in a tiny office with no natural light. As they take on a few more people they move into a small office space and celebrate the move. What typically tends to happen is these core people tend to create a 'culture' and set the rules of what is acceptable, especially how they communicate with one another. Keep in mind that this style of communication is often similar to that of a close group of friends, where the voice is often authentic.

As the organisation grows, each of the original group of people (those that stay on) take on new roles and responsibilities. Often these individuals step into senior management roles that require people management.

These new roles of heads of different departments, require the individual to somehow get comfortable with the new responsibilities that they may not be equipped to handle. The individual then begins to take on a persona and wear a mask that they feel they should for that particular position. When anyone begins to take on these typically hierarchically lead personas the way in which they communicate becomes inauthentic. This is the voice of the corporate world we all know. Imagine that this same business, with these new-formed communication styles and hierarchical habits grows over the course of say 10-15 years. They take on even more staff and are now an organisation that has between 70-100 staff. As a business they are making circa £4-£6m a year (US$6-US$9m a year), and have plans to take over the world. Yet for the last few years surpassing this level feels like an insurmountable hurdle.

As an organisation grows, be it nationally, regionally or internationally, the style of communication and organisational culture changes and morphs. The culture is dictated by the three people at the top. Very often these authoritarian communication styles and associated cultures do not work well, as cultural sensitivities of the countries you are expanding into have to be taken into account. The style of communication cannot necessarily have that 'dictator-esque' vibe to it; if it does, you will lose your best staff. You will not encourage the same level of commitment from your 50th employee as you had from your 5th (who probably now has a seat on the board of directors of your business and helped create this new authoritarian communication style).

I have heard some terrible things being said by business leaders; one of the worst things a business leader can say to their staff is, "We have always done it this way." When you hear such a statement from a business leader you can be certain that things are going to be challenging. This is most likely not due to the external market, but because there is a huge resistance to making the necessary adjustments to allow change. Without the adjustments, navigating over the hurdles will be impossible. You need to model change in order to grow. Blockbuster disappeared from the high street pretty quickly because of their inability to make the necessary adjustments to move with the times.

Each new generation of employees is different, and what was once accepted as the norm may no longer be accepted. People want to be respected and work in a place that cares for their wellbeing. It is seen as the entitled generation by some. I agree that we all had to work hard to earn respect and get to where we are now, yet there are young adults, a bit wet behind the ears, leaving university and entering the workforce, that have greater expectations and will not put up with being spoken to badly. There is a lot to learn from this new generation of people joining the workforce.

If your ethos as a business leader is that you have always done things a certain way and that's how it will stay and are not open to change, your business is likely to suffocate out of existence. The statement 'we have always done it this way' is so limiting to your staff. Imagine if the staff at Google were told *'this is how we have always done it, so keep your head down and just keep doing the task you have been assigned',* we would not have some of the most fascinating new technologies available to us, like 90% of the surface of the earth being mapped. From my experience and research, the organisations that are open to change, in order to become more efficient, productive and engaging with staff, will overcome their growth hurdles a lot quicker than an organisation that is rigid.

I understand that change is scary for some people; as you grow you will hire new people and potentially have new offices to accommodate the growing workforce. New staff and a new office location will bring additional challenges. New employees bring a new vibe and energy with them, people are relocated within the office to make space or fit into the new space, all of which mean that new routines must be created. The better you can help people create these new routines and give them time to adjust to one another, the greater the rewards. I remember during the last office move I was part of there were a few times I took the wrong turn on my way to work and drove on autopilot to the old office. I'd only realise when I was in the car park that I was in the wrong office. We are equipped to deal with change; after all, our brains are able to make new connections to form new habits, but it may take some time (as I discovered when I ended up in the wrong car park a couple of times).

Often the lack of communication and involvement from staff can make the changes that you wish to implement hard for people to adapt to, and there may be resistance.

The solution for this is to communicate effectively, communicate, communicate and communicate again. But there is a certain style of communication that is so important here. Put yourself in someone else's shoes and really understand how these changes will impact them and what is required of them. Show empathy to your staff regarding the disruption the changes will bring and what you, as the employer, will do to help minimise the impact on their daily work lives. The sales team I was a part of for many years was small. We had worked together for a long time and formed strong bonds with one another. There was a new person introduced into the mix and their integration needed some management. It was another big personality being added into a team of big personalities who all had very different communication styles.

As your business grows you will need more senior experienced staff. New recruits often threaten the status quo of the existing staff and you hired the new person for a reason. Make people aware as to the purpose of hiring this person and what they bring to the team. While in the interview process you thought this person would fit into the culture of the organisation. Keep in mind that your new hire comes with the skills you need, the experience you want and their own way of communicating. They will also be used to certain things from their last organisation that they feel are missing in yours. Take the time to get to know your staff and don't be afraid of the feedback they have for you. Ditch the defensiveness and listen with open curiosity. Often this is hard to do because you are one of the people who helped create the culture of the organisation that you are in, and it can often feel like a personal attack.

I recall a time when I was sitting with the MD of an organisation that I worked with and we were travelling to the airport to catch a flight together. I had been in this organisation only a short time at this point and wanted to share my initial thoughts, so we could work out a way of addressing some of the issues I had observed in the team and the organisation. What better time to get the MD's attention than this?

I made a comment about the things that I thought were great about the organisation, and mentioned that there were things that I thought could do with improvement and did not sit well with me. This comment was ignored so I parked it. I was certainly not going to let it go that easily because the issues had a very simple solution. I brought it up again on our flight back from seeing our client and prompted a little harder for a response from the MD, who had at the time very reluctantly and defensively asked me what the issues were. The defensiveness was clearly displayed on the MD's face and voice. The feedback I wanted to give was not a personal attack, it was an unbiased view of what needed fixing. Our discussion amounted to nothing; what could have been a very productive and open dialogue was shut down. I was hired to head up the largest billing account this organisation had, my role was to coach the team and get the most out of the account. This account had the highest staff turnover within the agency and was known to be the hardest account to work on, with the most demanding clients.

The CEO and MD of this organisation were so stuck in the hierarchical structure they had created, that feedback from a subordinate on what and how improvements could be made, was more often than not shut down.

When you hire senior staff and pay them a hefty salary, be open to receiving feedback from them. In fact I encourage you to actively ask for it. Internal feedback should be seen as just as valuable as client feedback. Addressing the root cause of some of the negative feedback given to you by your staff will benefit your organisation. It is definitely worth listening with a sense of curiosity in order to see the situation they are pointing out from the perspective of the person sharing the feedback. You have played a part in creating the future which now awaits you, and you are responsible for what you do next, and change it if need be. We have a collective responsibility to implement change and hold one another accountable for our tasks. If you see that something needs to change within your organisation then speak up. You owe it to yourself and your future to take that responsibility and create a new future that is possible with the right input from your team.

The power struggle and lack of willingness of some business leaders to be challenged and open to receiving valuable feedback is damaging to their business. The feedback highlights where improvements can be made to avoid a further loss of staff and unhappy clients. Staff loss is detrimental to organisations, clients like continuity; it takes your clients and you a lot of energy getting your operations and account management team up to speed on their business. If they do not get staff continuity and excellent service from you they will go elsewhere.

The business leaders I have worked with who are open to feedback and having an open and honest dialogue are the ones whose business does well. They overcome the hurdles and struggle their business encounters as soon as they arise.

They are willing to be flexible, take risks, and address the issues head on. Bury your head in the sand, and always do what you have always done, then you will get what you have always got. A business that runs on a hierarchical system of authoritarian communication, compliance and fear, leads to an increase in staff turnover and low productivity. Thriving businesses encourage collaborative, creative, empathetic and honest dialogue and discussion, which is the art of staying grounded within yourself and not losing your head.

Bringing out the humanity in human

Organisational leaders more often than not rely too heavily on the human resources department to deal with the people issues. I personally have a real issue with the term human resources. It is the plague of our times that many business leaders see humans as a commodity much like a bag of coffee beans or a drum of oil. Like with commodities, where we use 1.5 times the amount of resources that the planet can sustain, many organisations extract the same from their staff: 1.5 times the energy they have to give. What are we left with? A society that is so overworked and undervalued, zombies who drown their stress in destructive habits, like the sneaky bottle of wine to yourself, in front of the mind-numbing television. I will assume that your organisation holds an appraisal for its staff each year: once a year there is a formal process that allows '360 degree feedback'. In actual fact it is a stressful, pointless task to justify either giving or not giving someone a pay rise. Why do employees have to wait for 12 months to be given feedback, often by someone who has not taken the time to get to know them or has little to no human communication skills? This whole system that we have created seems absurd to me. Too few sustainable options come of these and documents are signed only to be put on file. I understand that there has to be a paper trail for everything, so you can tick off one more item that you have been compliant with; however, this should definitely not be a replacement for real human connections.

As people, we are taught a multitude of subjects at school and our family try to teach us right from wrong. The one thing we are not often taught is how to communicate with each other, we just pick this up as we go along. This self-taught communication changes depending on the roles we wish to play and you wouldn't think that poor communication could be the primary issue within your organisation. Poor communication if left unchecked can lead to a very serious issue which you can no longer ignore: bullying.

How is bullying addressed within your organisation? I cannot even count the number of times I have witnessed an organisation paying someone off to get rid of them rather than address the actual issues of bullying, to help both the bullies and the victims of bullying realise that their communication style needs adjustment in order to create a win-win outcome. It is easier to address what shows up at the surface than actually look at the root cause of the problems. Imagine if your gardener just went round the garden in spring and only snipped the weeds at a surface level, leaving the roots exactly where they are. When the roots are not fully dug up, the weeds are guaranteed to grow back. The gardener pulling up the roots does not guarantee of course that you will not have weeds in the garden again, but what it will do is stop that same weed from popping its head back up. Dealing with communication issues is very much the same. You need to address the root cause and teach individuals a better way of communicating with one another.

Having been on a few management training courses, two of the main focus points of the training agenda are: 1) how to get compliance and 2) how to get rid of someone. This getting rid of someone is disguised as a performance review or personal improvement plan (PIP). I refer to this HR policy and process as legalised emotional violence. When these issues arise, and you have put someone on a PIP, what you are in fact communicating to everyone within your organisation is that you have connected with someone on a superficial level. Of course you do have to make tough decisions, it is business after all, and you are in the business of making money. There may very well be no other way than to show someone the door. Before you do that, know that you have done all you could. Begin by looking at the root cause of the behaviour and see if you can connect with that individual from this place. It takes a lot of strength to connect with people at this level, this type of connection means being vulnerable. Being comfortable with vulnerability is tricky because it also means you have to connect to your humanness that is beyond your position, your wealth, your educational background and all the other things that are so tightly held with a sense of who you are.

If you are able to connect with individuals at this level, it will resonate with the humanity of the wider organisation, and create a better working environment. This will lead to easing the pressure cooker environments and lead to more compassionate communication. Hire and fire with thought and care.

In 2006, I had a colleague who used to work on my client campaigns; he had just left university and took a job as a telemarketer. When I left the organisation, he joined me at the new organisation also as a caller on more of my campaigns. This young man is as bright and witty as they come.

The Singapore office that the MD had recently set up needed a team leader to head up and train the callers in Singapore. I had encouraged him to apply, as I knew he was more than capable of doing so much more and this would be a great new challenge for this young lad. He was based in the Singapore office for several months. In his role, while he still made calls, he took on significantly more responsibility. In the absence of an operations director for Singapore, he filled that role.

After the several months stint in Singapore he returned to the London office and was put back into his role as a telemarketer even though he had just successfully run the entire calling team. Over time his once excellent work began to suffer. His motivation dropped and the programme managers found giving him direction really difficult. The programme managers he was now reporting to were relatively new and did not fully grasp the history and so did not know how to communicate with him or motivate him. He got put on a PIP and eventually he decided enough was enough and he left.

Sadly, the head of his department handled the communication with him particularly badly. Instead of nurturing this young man's talent, who went out to Asia having never been there before, and did such a superb job in a role he had never done before, they squashed out the spark. This story is not unique to this young man, it is something individuals experience each and every day. Instead of working on the root cause and helping improve the situation they only worked on the surface issues.

Celebrating the arrival of new employees is commonplace. After all, they have decided to work with you and your organisation, you won this one, which is another way you can stick two fingers up at your competition. Help each new arrival to really integrate into the company beyond the mandatory two-week induction process. Ensure the new starter gets one-to-one time with all the people you want them to associate with, and help them build bridges. Leverage their knowledge and experience to benefit your own organisation and team. There are bound to be a few things that can be learnt from new hires and taken on board in your organisation. If it will help make your business a better place to work and thus the money-making machine you want it to be, then implement it. Even if your new employee has no previous experience, it does not mean they do not have something of value to say; be open to asking and listening.

Most organisations are good at giving new hires mandatory induction training on systems and processes. Yet giving them the right training is rare. Training is also not refreshed, be it on skills, systems or processes. Don't assume anything; be willing to take the time to show people how to do something. Even if it is someone who has worked with you for years, apply the same rules of training to them too. Some organisations go as far as having their staff sit an 'exam' each year to test them on their services or product knowledge. You may not wish to go that far, but you do need to invest in their learning and topping up this knowledge.

Something that adds to the heat of the pressure cooker environment is that we are not taught how to deliver difficult messages with compassion. We often act on impulse and let off steam when we are angry and aren't necessarily our best self, leaving employees feeling humiliated and undervalued. The relationship you have with your staff is fragile, don't break the trust and goodwill you have generated. Put anger into perspective. What exactly has made you angry and what are you going to do about finding a solution to the problem? The more you let people in your organisation get away with communicating in such a non-connected way, the worse your internal pressure cooker will become.

Have difficult conversations, it is important to express when things are not right. I am suggesting that you teach people how to change the way the message is delivered and communicated. Deliver the message so that the other person involved is respected and communicated to with empathy, it makes the discussion generative. In order to have a generative conversation, both parties involved have to want to find a solution together and create something new. Often I see people deliver a difficult message in a manner that just wants to get it over and done with, not thinking about what can be done as a collective or how the person receiving the message will react. Leaders with poor communication skills and those who lash out aggressively at their employees, damage relationships. This breakdown in communication is a big reason for people to leave an organisation. Employers who behave in this manner will very often be left with skills gaps in their workforce, which means that growing the business will be an issue. Hiring the right staff is not only time consuming, it is also expensive.

> *Edward is the owner of a digital agency for whom I have the utmost respect. What makes this man stand out is the way in which he communicates with his team as a compassionate communicator. He had the hard task of firing someone and the way he did it was really kind and human. He had told the young woman he was firing the reason he had to let her go and offered to give her a reference.*
>
> *Unlike others in this organisation who would just go back to their work and pretend nothing had happened, Edward got his whole team into a meeting room and explained to them what had happened, to get their feedback on the situation.*
>
> *Knowing this departure would affect people, as the colleague being fired was well liked, he took it on board and then sent out an email to everyone within the organisation explaining the departure. He then took the time to walk around and speak to people about what had happened, without revealing the details of why. I will never forget his simple act of showing humanity, the way he handled this situation made people see him with new eyes and respect.*

What difficult situations do you face that could potentially be handled like Edward? Not only was Edward seen as being human, he also saved himself and the whole team precious time that would have otherwise have been lost to 'water-cooler gossip'.

The pains of mergers & acquisitions

Many organisations face issues in business growth and progress when they are in the midst of a merger or acquisition. Mergers & acquisitions (M&A) threaten employees with changes in organisational culture, potential redundancies and changes within the team. Maslow's hierarchy of needs highlights our very basic primal need for security. It is this basic need for security that when threatened brings out our most primitive survival state of the lizard brain. It kicks our fight or flight mechanism to be activated, and our ability to communicate with compassion gets flung out of the window. In times like these, compassionate communication should be a priority. Manage the change well, improve communication between you and your leadership team and help your leaders improve the communications with their teams. Keep people in the loop, and do what you can to ease their frustration. If you know that you need to let some people go, try going beyond the call of duty and see if any of your network are hiring, put in a good word if it is right to do so. If you are going to be the one walking away post M&A with a richer pocket, it is all too easy to disengage. Remember you still have people relying on you and a responsibility to the people who joined you, believed in your vision, to help fulfil your goals. Treat them well as it is a small world and you never know who you will bump into again. Don't burn your bridges with your teams, they are the leaders of the future and may very well be employing someone close to you.

The change in culture as a result of merging two teams should not be underestimated. Culture is something that must evolve along with us. Observe, learn and identify the cultural traits you wish to encourage and the ones you now have the opportunity to discourage.

All these things are huge hurdles for businesses to get over. People are sometimes so wrapped up in the strategy and which market to conquer next that it's easy to ignore what's happening in their own backyard. Fix the problems at home first and then go and take over the world. You will be in a stronger position to do so with the backing of a strong foundation that is maintained.

Communication styles

We are so afraid of humanity in the workplace and getting to the heart of any issue, because it means we have to confront our vulnerability which we spend so much effort trying to avoid. The current solution offered for better employee communication is to have someone come in and run psychometric testing prior to a training day. The issue with these tests is that while they are great at revealing so much about the individual's personality traits and preferences, the results do not offer sustainable or pragmatic solutions that solve the communication issues that people have, given that everyone's personality is unique.

Companies spend a lot of money using psychometric testing on staff and making them waste precious time completing personality test after personality test, only to never use the findings in a sustainable meaningful way. The tests are done with good intentions, each time there is a new trainer hired to 'fix' how people communicate. Sadly it is often a waste of precious time, not because personality testing is a waste of time, on the contrary, personality tests provide an incredible insight for an organisation/manager on their staff's working style or preference. What I do think is a huge waste of time and money is when this is all done, hardly any of the useful insights are used or communicated when teams are put together. I've always been told my own personality type and preferences. I am certain you know your own from the number of tests you may have completed in the past. If you don't know the results of the personality tests of your team, then make it your mission to find out and use it to build and keep a coherent, well-functioning team.

Imagine how productive your project teams could be if when they were chosen, each person knew the skills, personality preferences and styles everyone else brought to the table that could be leveraged to complete the task most efficiently. I mean really, why give minor detail work to someone who is a big picture person? That individual will only get frustrated and hold up the project delivery timeline. If I know that I am better suited than someone else to a particular task, I should then help take the task on from them or teach them how to do it. If you have spent money (personality tests are not cheap) on getting individual personalities profiled or tests done with your staff, then use the resulting information, encourage people to share their findings.

Many years ago I worked for a large publisher and was sent on a two-day management training course, where all the managers in the room had to fill in a very popularly used personality test. The test was done to find out what type of personality we each had. It was a lot of fun and we all had a giggle about our findings and did the whole "Oh I guessed as much" or "wow, who would've thought." We left the training day with the results printed out on a pretty piece of paper. That was that, aside from me knowing my own preferences, which I pretty much already knew. Not once after that training day did the director who I reported to ever use these results to arrange her team more efficiently or communicate with us in a way that would have been in keeping with the preference of her employees.

The best teams are structured in such a way that each person within the team has complementary skills to another. As the business leader, do a personality test of your own to understand your own preferences. This information will allow you to seek out and surround yourself with the best possible team to complement your skills and fill in skills that are not your forte.

There is a gentleman I know, Simon, who is the MD of a digital marketing agency and has this wonderful skill of intuitively knowing the specific type of person and what experience that person needs to have to join his team. Each senior hire he has made complements his skill set and fills in the 'gaps'. He has a strong leadership team who work very well together, like a well-oiled machine.

The reality is that deadlines and juggling multiple projects is stressful. It does seem like a waste of energy to add to that stress by putting the wrong team together in the first place or not communicating individuals' strengths to the whole team. Once a team is made aware of what specific skills their colleagues bring to the table, they can set up projects and subteams in such a way that allows each person to make the most their strengths. This type of organising takes efficient communication and good leadership skills. It is only when we are able to implement good communication practices and put the right team together from the start that we can reduce the impact of the pressure cooker environment.

- What are the struggle zones in your business?

  _____

  _____

  _____

- What are the current team dynamics?

  _____

  _____

  _____

- How would you like your business to look?

  _____

  _____

  _____

- What specifically needs to change?

  _____

  _____

- What can you and will you change?

  _____

  _____

- How can you bring more humanity into certain situations?

  _____

  _____

  _____

- Who will be involved in the process of implementing the changes?

  _____

  _____

  _____

- How will you implement the changes?

  _____

  _____

  _____

- How do you monitor the implementation?

  _____

  _____

  _____

Chapter 2:
Make humanity a priority and be a compassionate leader

It may be strange at first to hear the words love and compassion used within the context of business. Compassion and love are most commonly associated with close personal relationships and religious teachings. Love and compassion are the basic factors we require as humans to thrive as they are at the core of our very essence. We are all part of society and there is a fundamental need for humanity to be a priority.

In order to create healthy balanced relationships based on compassion, you have to start with having this type of relationship with yourself. When you are in balance with yourself, you can begin to connect in a more meaningful and genuine way with other people.

We can see this lack of balance, connection, compassion and love play out in our world on a macro level. In the last five months (since November 2015) there have been horrific attacks in France, Mali, Tunisia, Indonesia, Burkina Faso, Somalia, Turkey, Ivory Coast, Belgium and Pakistan. These attacks have been by people who are hell-bent on terrorising anyone and everyone who disagrees with their opinions/ viewpoints and they ultimately want control. They show little to no respect for humanity or human life. There needs to be a shift in their thinking as people and they need to make humanity a priority over power or control.

It gives us a clear indication that the way we relate and communicate to one another can be destructive. In order to impact on a macro level you have to start at the micro level, which in this case is within your business. How are you supposed to impact anything at a global level if you are unable to even address the fundamental issues within your immediate environment? The master-slave fashion of communicating we have become accustomed to, because it does not work. We have to become part of the solution. We have to stand up and take responsibility for the decisions that were made either by us or others that we did not stand up to, to empower the people around us so we in turn become empowered to pursue the things that matter.

Otto Scharmer, a senior lecturer at MIT on the u-Lab course, talks about the three points of view when it comes to addressing the root cause of disruption:

1. Keep muddling through with the same old way of doing things, exactly as we have always done.

2. Move apart as people in our fear and disagreement behind walls that are there to keep us apart.

3. Take responsibility and move together towards something new, like the tearing down of the Berlin Wall.

The solution is for all of us to move towards encouraging a culture of compassionate communication and create something new. You, as the business leader, are in a great position to lead this change and bring about an evolution in the business world, starting within your own organisation. Engaging with employees at the most basic level of humanity and connection which in turn drives commitment, rather than leading from a place of compliance and fear. The challenge is to look at yourself and your decisions in the mirror, metaphorically standing naked as the day you were born. Know your part in creating the future which now awaits you and what you want to create and have awaiting you the next time you take stock of where you are. The process of self-awareness can be harder for some than others. Your journey to knowing yourself is a unique one, no two will be the same. Some people are more in touch with their humanity than others. Taking down the barriers and confronting your limiting beliefs can be as liberating as it is frightening, so be patient and give yourself the necessary time to do so.

We are not taught at school how to communicate; from the moment we begin to observe the world around us we are filled with messages of prejudice and have beliefs instilled in us that take us away from our natural need to love and have compassion. There is a huge culture of 'I': what I want, and what I need and what I am going to do, with little thought to the collective 'we', what is best for the collective, all of 'us'. Don't get me wrong, there is nothing wrong with 'I' and 'me';

but as with everything in life there must be some balance. My mind boggles at how out of balance we are. There are over 7 billion people on this planet and in an article by *The Guardian* newspaper in 2014, 1% of the world's population has half of the wealth. That leaves the other 99% to fight over the remaining half.

As mentioned previously, we're consuming 1.5 times what the planet can sustain. This is a real issue and should be a concern for everyone. Everyone wants to secure something for oneself and one's family, it is important to us, otherwise we would not exchange our life hours for money. Our life on this planet is finite, so make this life that you have been given count. The answer is not for us to kill one another or stab one another in the back to have financial security or a nicer car than the guy that lives next door. The key to our success is working together, as a collective, to help and support one another.

Now imagine for a minute that we could create a world where people came to work happy or at the very least content. Where everyone knew they were working towards a goal, from which everyone benefits. A place of work where people speak to one another compassionately and difficult conversations are had in a way that are generative instead of being destructive. Perhaps this is too far from our current reality for us to conceive; however, it is possible to take small steps towards creating a better environment.

In July 2005 I lost a dear friend in the London bombings, but it has not waivered my faith in humanity and my knowing that we have strength when we stand together. Unfortunately the government we elected decided for us that we would go to war, completely disregarding all the peaceful protests in the streets and in doing so created an even bigger threat and problem. Continuing with this type of behaviour will only create even more problems in the heart of it all; it does not take into account humanity. Our collective heart and soul is damaged each time an innocent person dies. There are situations in work that are as disruptive and cause emotional pain to you, the people who work for you and with you. I believe in the power of humanity and compassion to help bring about transformation.

Creating a better environment and world is not a fantasy. There are businesses that put their employees front and centre (for example: Google, Innocent Drinks, Ben & Jerry's), they make great profits and invest it back into the people who work for them. They have created business cultures that they can be proud of. The model they have adopted is driven by customers' demands for a happy emotional story, to justify making a purchase and to set a benchmark. Bringing humanity into the mainstream works, and there should be nothing stopping you from becoming the benchmark in your own industry.

Self-awareness

A greater self-awareness is fundamental in beginning the process of change and embracing compassionate communication. We don't take much time in our busy lives to stop and take stock of the things that are important. We don't even know ourselves very well, with all the masks we have to wear, depending on the role we are asked to play at any given time in our life. We often lose our authentic self and voice in the process. We only focus on the traits that get us what we want. We have little conscious awareness as to what our values, beliefs and personality traits both 'bad' and 'good' are. Our awareness is limited to what is on the surface, because this is what we are shown as being acceptable. In order for anything to grow, transform and be a better version of what it was before, we have to look deeper. Freud's iceberg metaphor eludes that approximately 90% of our behaviours are driven by things hidden beneath the surface (our unconscious mind). This includes our belief systems that can be updated (as has been shown by various therapeutic interventions), which means the whole system can change.

This section of the book is mainly made up of exercises/tasks to help you get to know yourself better. Through knowing yourself better, you are able to acknowledge your 'humanness' and it is through this process I find most people organically have improved self-expression. Once you recognise and slowly begin to accept all the complex parts of you, you will start to see other people's perspective with empathy and, I hope, with acceptance.

Task 1: The alphabet of me

In this task you will highlight your 'good' and 'bad' attributes, then you should be able to look at both sides of the alphabet table and acknowledge that you are both 'this' and 'that', and much more. I have put the words good, bad, positive and negative in inverted commas throughout, because in reality what may be seen as a negative trait can be seen as positive in the right context and vice versa.

The purpose of this exercise is that in order to be a compassionate leader, you must first accept yourself for you 'warts and all' and only then will you be able to 'see' someone else and accept that they too are also both 'this' and 'that'. Acceptance and acknowledgement allows us to be more human and not set unrealistic expectations for ourselves or judge so harshly. It may in fact highlight areas you might like to better. The majority of business leaders and owners I know are really tough on themselves. They often set very high standards and expectations; this is so stressful for them and it leaves no room for error, and like me, I am sure there is some truth in this for you too.

Completing the table may take some time. It took me a week to complete and I found it challenging. It's not necessarily easy to put down on paper the things that you would rather hide from view from other people and yourself. I certainly faced some of my own internal resistance when I did this task. Perhaps for you it will be different. This is an adapted version of a task that was set for me by my brand consultant Jenny Andersson (at the start of a branding exercise I was doing with her), and an exercise from a *'hero's journey'* weekend workshop I attended with Robert Dilts.

The task that Jenny had set me was to fill out a lexicon of me from A-Z, and write down all my 'positive' attributes. As I began this exercise, I added a whole second column of my 'negative' attributes. It was at first hard for me to be so honest and vulnerable to myself, I called it my table of acceptance.

The first stage of this task is for you to complete your own table of acceptance and then have everyone in your team complete one too. The purpose of this exercise is not to humiliate or put anyone down, it is purely for a greater self-awareness. It is an exercise that will push you and your team out of your comfort zone.

Write down in the space below or make a copy of the table. Insert next to each letter a word that best describes you. Don't filter or sugar-coat or find reasons as to why, just write down what best fits how you see yourself. Go with your gut instincts for this. If you can't think of words for some letters just leave them out. Please do try to fill out both sides of the table and if you are the type of person who feels they have no 'negatives' then maybe ask someone who is willing to be honest with you.

Here are a few examples from my own table of acceptance to get you going.

Action-oriented & Angry
Bright & Blunt
Compassionate & Challenging
Empathetic & Emotional
Determined & Daring

The 'Positive'	The 'Negative'
A	A
B	B
C	C
D	D
E	E
F	F
G	G
H	H
I	I
J	J
K	K
L	L
M	M
N	N
O	O
P	P
Q	Q
R	R
S	S
T	T
U	U
V	V
W	W
X	X
Y	Y
Z	Z

Some time ago I went to a seminar that Robert Dilts, the founder of NLP University, was speaking at. One of the exercises that we had to complete was that everyone in the room had to pick a partner to work with and sit opposite them. The exercise was an exercise on accepting. Each person had to say one thing about themselves they liked and one thing about themselves they didn't like. The person sitting opposite them had to repeat back to them what they had said, but adding the following words: "I see that you are.......... (*fill in the blank with the 'negative' trait) and I see that you are .... (fill in the blank with a 'positive' trait) and you are so much more." This exercise is then repeated to the other person.*

For the second part of this task, take your filled-in sheet (it doesn't matter if you have some letters left blank), read each word you have written down out loud and say to yourself in the mirror or to someone else:

"I am .... (fill in the blank with something from the first column) AND I am...... (fill in the blank with something from the second column) AND I am so much more."

This exercise is predominantly about acceptance, but it is also awareness and knowledge you have the power and the choice of when and how to use these traits. None of the traits are 'good' or 'bad', it's how and when you use them that make it so.

You can keep going with this exercise until you have gone through everything you have written down in your table of acceptance. It is likely to challenge your sense of vulnerability opening yourself up like this to another person. If you are doing this task with someone else, encourage them to repeat their table of acceptance words to you.

Task 2: (optional) The eulogy

Writing a eulogy can be a very painful task. So don't push yourself to do the task, it is optional. You are to write two eulogies for yourself as though you have passed on. If you can face doing it, it's a wonderful thing to be able to do, because it will help you visualise the changes that you need to make in order to create the life you want for yourself.

The first eulogy is based on the person you are now and what you have done up until this point, and be brutally honest, this exercise is for you and only you. The second is based on the person you have the potential to become, using your new-found gift of self-awareness to leave a legacy you can be proud of. The person who is self-aware, compassionate and open hearted. The second eulogy is based on how you would like to be remembered by the people who work for you, by your children, by your friends and loved ones who care for you.

I understand the task may seem quite morbid or challenging to some. The only things guaranteed in our life are taxes and death. We only get one shot at this life, and we have a chance to make a difference for more than just ourselves, so make it count. It is the selfish way we have been living and working that has created the problems we now face. Only we have the power to fix the problems that our disconnection from: oneself, one another and our environment, through the choices we make.

I suggest that you keep each eulogy to one/two pages at most. And if you don't want to write that much, just write down the main bullet points. If you are more visual then draw a representation of each eulogy.

Once you have completed the two eulogies, look at the differences between the two and highlight them. What are the first three things you will do differently from this very moment to get your real eulogy when the time comes to sound and look how you want to be remembered? Start with things that you know you can actually implement and follow through with, ideally something that will really help you connect with your deeper sense of humanity and compassion.

I also suggest you share the changes you will implement with someone you trust and will help hold you accountable for making these changes. It is never too late to care.

Task 3: Calm the inner critic

I perhaps should have titled this chapter self-acceptance and not self-awareness. Yet to be self-accepting if you are not fully self-aware is hard. One thing I find very sad is the level of judgment and criticism that is used when we speak to ourselves, let alone other people. Knowing how you speak to yourself makes it easier to notice how you speak to others.

Take notice of how you speak to yourself (the tone, the volume, the pace and the tempo) and what you say (the content of the message). Do you speak to yourself in a way you would want someone to speak to your child or another person you love dearly?

I have noticed over the years that through my awareness of how my inner critic speaks to me, I have become more aware of how I speak to other people. It has allowed me to make a conscious shift in my tone, volume and pace, which ultimately shifts my behaviour and it changes how I feel about the person I am speaking to and avoids what could have been a difficult situation. If I consciously ease my pace, tone and volume I take the edge off an otherwise difficult situation and things become easier to handle. This takes a significant amount of practice but is definitely possible. Start first with noticing your inner critic and begin to consciously change that. After all, it is your *own* voice, and you have full control over your own voice.

Once you have practised adjusting the way you speak to yourself a few times, doing so with other people becomes easier. After all, if you won't allow someone else to speak to your loved one in that manner, why do you talk to yourself in that way?

I ran a workshop some time ago on mindfulness. One of the participants was a 6 feet 4 tall man, well educated and a tough leader. He had been running his company for 16 years. I ran a version of the second and third tasks as listed above in the workshop. We all came back together to discuss what we found out about ourselves, and what we were going to change going forward. This gentleman broke down in floods of tears from doing these tasks, from a deep sadness that he was not fully in touch with his humanity. All he was focusing on was getting the numbers in, not consciously thinking about the cost to him, his staff, his family or his health. He made some significant changes in his life: he now works several hours less a week and makes time for his family, and gives his staff more flexibility. He's reported that his employees have commented on how he seems calmer, and he is achieving better sales numbers than he ever had before.

Awareness of the other

To be a great leader you must know the people you lead. It is not easy to find out someone's true feelings (YES! I said feelings in a business book. Get over it!), you are human and whether you like it or not you are stuck with these pesky things called feelings. The world of business as we know it has taught each of us, you included, that you have to be what someone expects of you. You have to fit into their idea of what is 'right', wave the corporate flag and not push the boss or question them. In times of political, financial and social insecurity people do whatever they can and need to in order to hold on to the very thing that feeds them and keeps a roof over their head: their job. The impact of this is that no one will rock the boat and say what's really going on under the surface. People will say whatever they need to, to keep you at arm's length.

Being a compassionate leader also means encouraging better behaviours and habits within your team. To do that you must understand what drives people:

- What are the goals they have for their life?

- What do they want their eulogy to say?

- What is important to them?

- What do they value?

- What are their beliefs?

- How can you support them in the role they are in to develop the qualities and skills to help them get to that goal?

I encourage you at this stage to get your teams to complete the self-awareness tasks for themselves and see what changes it may organically bring forth in them. In order to really know someone else you have to walk a mile in their shoes. Until you can see and feel yourself in someone else's shoes, you are not really able to show empathy, and that as a compassionate leader is an essential skill.

I sat in on an appraisal of one of the account directors in my team, Anna, and one of her direct reports, the senior account manager, Emily. I have never before had to bring an appraisal to a halt halfway through and have it rescheduled. I wanted the appraisal process to be as positive as it could be for both of these people, so it had to come to a stop. I knew full well they had been having issues. Emily had been filling in the role of both account manager and account director for a few months before Anna had been hired and was desperate for a promotion. Emily thought that she could do the account director's job and didn't see what value Anna had brought to her. Anna was unhappy with Emily treating her with contempt and not letting work go.

This situation happens all the time when there are changes to a team; in the end people get so disillusioned with the process and become disgruntled. The other key factor that added to the issue between these two is that the organisation had grown and changed over the last few years and the long-serving core team were friends and had no idea how to relate to new people. You don't have to be friends with someone to work well with them, but you DO have to be respectful and professional. If you like each other that is an added bonus and makes the office an easy place to be.

After rescheduling the appraisal I did a very simple coaching exercise with each of them separately, that you can easily replicate. This is a neuro-linguistic programming (NLP) exercise called perceptual positioning and I'm sure you will find it very useful. It simply is allowing yourself to change perspective by changing your position. Here's how it's done.

I had asked Emily to imagine it was the day of the original appraisal which I called to an early close. She had to sit the same way and really feel as though she was there, seeing and hearing everything she saw and felt that very moment. It was obvious to see her get to that place easily. Her body tensed up and her breathing became shallow. I wanted Emily to tell me what was going on with her physically and emotionally as she was saying the things she was saying to her account director. She then had to step out of her shoes and into the position of an observer, and make observations of what she 'saw' herself, in position one of self, was doing. How was her posture, how did she sound, and any other observations.

I then asked her to step into position two, and pretend to be Anna receiving the messages that Emily was giving. Emily had to sit like Anna and take on the persona of being Anna in all the details of that previously unsuccessful meeting, to really step into being this person. As Anna, what does she see and feel and hear when Emily, in position one, is saying, the things she said to Anna (who Emily was now pretending to be) during the meeting? This exercise is to really look at what resources you have that you can use the next time in order to ease a difficult situation. It allows you to experience you, from someone else's perspective. You will never know how that person really felt, but you can get a really good idea of things by stepping into their shoes.

I then asked Emily to step back into the role of the observer and asked her to look at what was going on in that interaction and make some observations. She certainly had some insight into how her behaviour was perceived, she felt real empathy for Anna, and was more aware of how she came across. I asked Emily to think of what she could do differently in that situation if it was replayed. The difference she could bring in her body language, in how she was sitting, or breathing, or the pace and tone she may have been using. What resourceful gift could she give herself in that interaction, and in doing so indirectly give a gift to Anna too?

The next step in this exercise was for Emily to step back into herself now with the new insights and resources she could bring in herself to have helped that interaction be less 'painful' and more positive for everyone involved. Emily was then able to see how she felt differently, she was able to bring this new quality into the conversation from the perspective of position one (the self) and then from position two (the other) again to verify that this indeed had changed how Emily thought Anna would also experience this interaction. I also ran this same perceptual positioning exercise with Anna, with much the same reactions and results I got with Emily.

The day of reckoning came about, the rescheduled appraisal. If I am being honest, I was worried we would get into that room and things would just descend back into that place of fighting for recognition, and one-upmanship. We were all sitting in a meeting room again and what a result! They both still said what they had to say to each other, but in a way I call generative. Some of the issues were not resolved, but what did happen is that instead of virtually throwing accusations at one another and getting defensive, they were able to remain calm and centred. They saw things from *each other's perspective and had empathy for where the other was coming from and had made some agreements; they found solutions to some of the issues. This is the start of compassionate communication. They took responsibility for themselves and what they could each do differently.*

It was a tricky dynamic for me to work with Emily and Anna. There was a real power struggle in the first appraisal and the added tension of having different communication styles, given their stark difference in cultural backgrounds. The dynamics that had previously caused so much drama were able to be resolved and in fact were no longer an issue. They were able to relax into themselves. They had more awareness of the collective and together created something better.

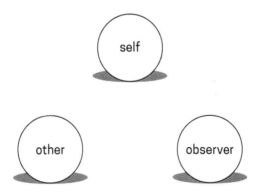

It is in the position of the observer that we
can identify what resources we need

If you want to get the most out of your interactions with people, try your best to be the observer. See things not only from your own perspective but also the other's perspective and work out what you can change in your interaction that may make this better for both of you.

Something you can relate to is perhaps a row with your significant other; if neither of you takes the first step to better the situation, through communication and understanding, things escalate and never really get resolved. We all have an inner child that just wants to love and be loved and our adult ego just wants to have the last word.

Accept vulnerability

All healthy growing relationships require us all to be vulnerable. Vulnerability allows people to see our humanity. When we show our vulnerability it allows us to be more honest and open in our communication. There is a joy to communicating with people. I am not by any means suggesting that you share with anyone at work all the sordid details of things that happened to you in your childhood. What I am saying is that the barrier of 'this is me with my friends and family' and 'this is me at work' has to be made a little shorter. You absolutely should keep boundaries, but the walls you put up need to be low enough so you can say hello over the wall and occasionally have a chat over a cup of tea. Make your personal boundary lines more like the ones between all of the countries of mainland Europe, and less like Mexico and the USA, or India and Pakistan. For compassion to develop within you, your organisation, your family, your community etc. you must give time, energy and effort to making it so. Don't let it die like the last project group you set up and had all of three meetings about. You know the one, the great idea and project that amounted to nothing. For anything to develop in this world, one must give time, energy and effort. I don't believe in this silly notion of work/life balance. It is all life and we must balance where we spend our energy and what we give our attention to.

Your vulnerability will allow you to open yourself up to a real connection to people. This is very scary for some because there is the fear of 'I am vulnerable and I will get hurt'. Yes, it is a real possibility and it is also a real possibility that you might find real joy in connecting with another human being. I do not mean romantically, but a connection of humanity and to collaboratively generate something new. There is real strength in showing vulnerability.

We are part of a world that is changing, and you have to be the revolutionary, the one that lights the way for compassionate leadership to be the norm in the workplace. For this to happen you have to become comfortable with and accept your vulnerability. In a world where compassionate communication is the norm, we can all begin to experience a new quality of human connection within business. The path taken by Nelson Mandela, Mahatma Gandhi, Malcom X and Martin Luther King was not easy. It was their vulnerability, strength and compassion that brought about change. They led people to create huge shifts in the world. Our compassion and strength need not match the great leaders of our time to have an impact; it is the simple acts of compassion that can make a big difference.

Here's a story of how the compassion of one woman helped me along my own journey and she doesn't even know it. I worked for a marketing consultancy, in their UK HQ. The head of my department came across as a rather aloof woman. She was really smart and people respected her for her knowledge and yet she wasn't the most approachable. In my second year of working there, the terrible bombings happened in London. Several bombs went off and people lost their lives and for a while everything was a blur. As I mentioned before, I sadly lost a friend of mine on that tragic day, he was on the tube to work going through King's Cross station. This news was the straw that proverbially broke the camel's back. I was already having a hard personal time of things. It was a time of reassessing what was important and looking at what I really wanted from my life. I felt I needed time to reassess and went to ask the 'big boss lady' if I could have a month off, so I could take some time out. My palms were sweaty and I anticipated her saying no. Instead her response utterly amazed me. She let her barriers down, she was merely human. For the first time in two years I saw her vulnerability and love.

She told me a story of how she had a long time ago lost someone very dear to her in a tragic accident, she understood what I was going through and was happy for me to take the time off that I needed. She even shed a tear. I will never forget how I felt that day. That someone gave me permission to see their vulnerability and humanity. In my eyes I had even more respect for this woman; this time it wasn't because of her knowledge, it was because of the person she is. I have never been more committed to working for anyone than I was her. I left the company soon after she did as I no longer felt that sense of loyalty once she had gone.

If you ever read comics as a child or watched any superhero movies, you know that even superheroes have vulnerabilities. There may be someone lurking in the shadows waiting to exploit an opportunity to 'take you down', but there are just as many people waiting for you to show them who you are so they can offer you commitment and loyalty. Life is not a comic, but we do have real heroes for us to aspire to become. Heroes that inspire from you dedication, commitment and loyalty, and are the type of people for whom you are happy to invest energy and time.

You run a business and you need individuals to perform the tasks you pay them to do. This exchange of money for time and task completion when run as a mechanical function is soul destroying. There is a huge need for greater compassion at work and in the way we interact with one another. We all wish to feel valued and to have a purpose, it is what drives us all.

- What resistance did you feel when doing these exercises?

  _____

  _____

- What impact did completing these exercises have on you?

  _____

  _____

- What changes can you implement that will have the biggest positive impact?

  _____

  _____

- What stops you from being vulnerable?

  _____

  _____

- What can you do to change the things that stop you or get in your way?

  _____

  _____

- How can being more self-aware benefit you and your team?

  _____

  _____

- How can being more compassionate benefit you and your team?

  _____

  _____

Chapter 3:
The rewards
of listening

Newton's first law of thermodynamics states that energy cannot be created or destroyed, it can only change from one form into another; the flow of heat is a form of energy transfer. Everything around us is made of energy, atoms and molecules that rotate and vibrate, only we do not see it. To the naked eye things look solid. We share this life force and energy with everyone around us; we just don't necessarily see it. There are things we can see and experience and it is those things that we can use to improve how we communicate with one another.

No one is perfect and there are people who do things in a manner that holds the basic principles of humanity at its core. I remember a time when I had just left university and had very little money. I was temping as a medical secretary for £10 (US$14.18) an hour and had not yet been paid *for the week. It was winter and I was at Liverpool Street station, with £3 (US$4.25) in my pocket and my train ticket home. I had just spent my £3 (US$4.25) on food and I noticed a young homeless lady sitting outside the station, asking people for money for a night at a hostel. I didn't have any money left, so I instead asked if she would like to share my meal with me, and I stopped to chat.*

She cried and thanked me, saying it was the kindest thing someone had done for her in a long time. She told me that people spat at her, someone even came over to kick her and one man threatened to burn her. This simple act of sharing my meal, and taking the time to talk with this young lady and listen to her story, made her day a little better and made me feel good about myself. I am sharing this story simply to illustrate that if we stop and listen to people, I mean really hear what they are saying with their words, expressions and gestures, not only can we enrich our own life, we can also help them.

It is respectful to actively listen to someone and it helps them feel like what they have to say is important. I have sat in meetings with people who love the sound of their own voice, they never stop talking, it is boring and feels worse than watching paint dry! I also come from a family who are loud. We all have a terrible habit of talking over each other most of the time, it's a miracle any conversation ever finishes. It's taken me a long time to learn how to ask someone a question and shut up. If I can learn to do this, with my family background, then anyone can! I have also lived in Britain for more than three-quarters of my life, and learning to communicate the polite British way has been hard going. It is, however, incredibly rewarding. I was genuinely amazed by how much more information people give you if you just ask them one question, shut up and wait patiently for the answer.

Try listening without judgment, which is harder to do than say, seeing how much we all like to be judgmental. Free your head from queuing up another question before the other person has finished talking. If you allow information to just come in, give it time to settle and for you to fully understand it, then you can gather any further valuable information. Great sales people and therapists have this skill nailed. It is a skill we all need to cultivate in order to really hear what people are saying. Once you have mastered this skill you will be able to uncover so much valuable information, for example to really find out about people's thoughts on your business and what needs improvement.

In order to create a better working environment, you should start getting information on what your employees think of the business culture you have created. Your employees are tasked with taking your business to the next level and you want to keep and develop your talent to drive success. Therefore there is a need to look at the culture you have created and work on evolving that. When you hear critical feedback of you or your business, it is hard not to take it personally and let it get to you. I have seen business leaders lash out in a really ugly way when told things they don't want to hear, when they have to admit they were wrong, or there is something they don't know or have done incorrectly. The advice I give on this is to allow people space to share their thoughts and, more importantly, give you space to process the information. It is hard to get feedback that isn't praise. Most business leaders usually have huge egos that stop them wanting to get feedback. There is always going to be someone/ groups of people who want to put you down. Despite that, listen as an observer and analyse the information as it may be useful.

When the feedback we receive is less than desirable, we don't necessarily want to hear it. What typically happens is that our lizard brain is activated and usually results in us behaving defensively. Even this instinctual response can be changed with practice. It is OK to dislike someone even if it is for no reason. It most definitely is NOT OK to disrespect, degrade or humiliate anyone. Often people have no idea they are potentially damaging someone else's self-esteem. As a business leader, try not to use the boss card when you want to throw your toys out of the pram. Using the boss card at work can often be as damaging to your relationships with your team as using the word divorce in an argument with your spouse is damaging to your relationship, instead of trying to resolve the real issues.

Early in my career I was taught the importance of preparation. *Know what you want to get out of a conversation, and tell the client about how wonderful the company you work for is and how great the solutions are.* In retrospect, I'm not entirely certain that was the best advice to give anyone in sales/customer service. I would go into meetings with a list of questions jotted down in preparation. I'd put together a great presentation and rehearsed it a million times; I had done all the background reading on who I was meeting and the company they worked for; I knew (well I thought I did anyway) their offering, their clients and their competitors. It was textbook preparation, rather foolishly I felt particularly smug that I was prepared for meetings. I learnt the hard way that while 'Business 101' states 'always be prepared' (and you should be, within reason), the first thing I should have been taught was to LISTEN.

I would ask clients the questions I so cleverly crafted, and before they were even done answering, I would mentally start running through my next question. By doing this I was missing little golden nuggets of information the client would be sharing with me, because I wasn't really fully there with them. I am ashamed to admit there were times back in those days when I was in my first job where I would be sitting with someone and let my judgmental mind disrupt how I spoke with them. Also I paid little attention when listening to them like a stereotypical estate agent might do. I managed to hit my financial targets but something was missing, my connections were transactional and superficial. Through trial and error, I learnt the value and wonder of listening actively. I started to step into people's business issues and their personal blocks in order to help them identify all the areas I could help with. There is such a thing as being overprepared; our research can create preconceptions and judgments. Our need (well mine certainly) to come across as 'clever' in order to show off and act like the big kahuna can get in the way of our ability to listen.

You can learn to give yourself the permission to really hear and see new perspectives. The change of perspective challenges your assumptions. It is this, the challenge to your assumptions, which will help you ask the right questions to discover what the real problems are. It helps to uncover what is really at the base of the iceberg and give the customer (internal or external) exactly the best solution for them that you can offer. If it means passing on business to someone else then so be it. The customer is not likely to forget your honesty and help. Sometimes the very client you send elsewhere comes back to you, with an even bigger project.

I recall one particular time, following several calls with a prospective client (a very large telecommunications organisation in Scandinavia) that I had been hunting for some time to get some work with, I had finally got hold of someone particularly senior there, Hans, we had a lengthy discussion about his requirements (I had already learnt how to actively listen by this point). I ended up advising Hans to use a different consultancy for the specific work he was looking to have done. This was an area that the other agency had a specialisation in and we only had a junior analyst for this subject matter.

Hans thanked me for my honesty, went away, and he resurfaced six months later asking for me by name to thank me for the recommendation. He let me know they were very happy with the work they had commissioned with the other agency. Great, but where was he going with this? I had still lost out on selling him a 12-month subscription to some research for £12,000 (US$18,000). He had, in fact, called to let me know that he was now looking at running a significantly larger consulting project in an area I had previously told him we did have expertise in and wanted to know if we would be interested in helping him. Research was to be done into the Middle Eastern and South African markets, he wanted us to meet with him and his marketing *team to discuss the project and provide a quote for the work. This initial project was worth £150,000 (US$225,000), which was significantly better than the first sum I was angling for, and by the end of 12 months they were my biggest billing client.*

When the first project was done, we had all gone out for a celebratory lunch. Over lunch I asked Hans what made him come back to us as we were certainly not the only company or the cheapest to complete this project for him. His response delighted me, most of all for the look on my then director's face (as he had previously reprimanded me for sending the client to the other agency to begin with). Hans said that of all the people he had spoken to about his specific requirements for that initial project, I was the only one who really listened and dug to understand the requirements and had been honest with him about the company's position and where he would be best suited to go.

Had I not actively listened out for the issues fully and offered him the best advice, he would not have remembered nor come back to work with an organisation who valued honesty, transparency and great customer service. If I had only used my strict rigid questions and hadn't allowed myself to really understand the issue, I would have only closed a £12,000 (US$18,000) research subscription deal. He may have done the project with us and lost the company the potential of getting any future business from this client, and damaged not only my reputation but also that of the company I worked for. So my decision was based on what was best for the client and what was in the best long-term interest of the company. NOT ALL BUSINESS IS GOOD

> *BUSINESS. One must be willing to say no to business if it doesn't make sense. You can only do this if you really listen and allow the information provided to guide your questions.*
>
> *Providing the best and right solution should be the priority. Even if Hans and his team hadn't come back to me, I knew that I had created a champion of the company I represented within this telecommunications organisation.*

I mentioned earlier that sales people typically start conversations knowing what they want to get out of them. This is true of most business leaders too. They are driven by financial reward and getting the necessary signature on the dotted line. The difference between a good sales person and a great sales person is that great sales people don't only go into conversations thinking *What can I get out of this?* They go into discussions thinking *How can we collectively find a solution to the client's problem that is mutually beneficial? How do we create something new and of value together?* It is a change of mindset from thinking of me to thinking of *us* as a collective. Once you are able to do this, you will open up discussions to new possibilities of creativity and innovation. Extending this same courtesy of the collective *us* mindset to your own employees/team creates new options. It is more than just a win-win scenario. I gave Hans the advice to go elsewhere because I knew it would really be what was best. I still had my target to hit, and I knew full well that turning down this chance of selling something in that moment would mean that I would have to work harder to hit that target. I just wasn't willing to compromise my own principles just to get a deal closed.

Listen with all your senses

This refers to also using your eyes and other senses to pick up on the nonverbal messages people give. To listen actively you must fine tune your ability to observe and pick up cues from the voice as well as the content. Notice the subtle differences as people speak: the pace, the tone and the volume. If the differences between what is normal for that person and what you are hearing are noticeable, then maybe you want to ask about it. Do not make your own assumptions or attach your own meaning to how someone is saying something. It is always best to just ask. Obviously don't question everything that is different or it may feel a bit like The Spanish Inquisition. At the end of a conversation, if there has been a more prominent tone, pace etc. and you feel it is relevant then ask about it.

When we speak we give off a 'vibe' to people. This vibe can be described as the subtle nonverbal information your body is giving out all the time. When you start listening in this way, you begin to pay more attention to people's facial expressions as they speak. I look out for any twitches they may have, what expression they are holding, taking a conscious mental note of the subtle and obvious changes that are going on as they speak to you. This process is to teach us to be more engaged and keep our minds active in the process of listening to take in all the information that is being presented. The purpose of it all is really simple: to be present with the other person and stepping into the world as they see it or describe it free of judgment.

The body is very fascinating; you can try and fool someone with your words and even voice but it is harder to betray someone with your body language. Have you ever noticed that someone may be verbally saying something that is in conflict with what their body is saying? For example, telling you they are really listening to you but their entire body is turned towards something obviously far more interesting. When someone speaks to you, notice their body language too. What happens as they speak? How do they hold their body when they speak to you vs. when they speak with someone else? If the body language doesn't match the verbal communication, it is worth trying to uncover if there is any reason behind it. Yes, there is a lot to remember; the more practice you get in doing this, the easier it becomes, the effort is worth it.

A few years ago, I was sitting in a large boardroom with my then MD and several people from a large prospective client. This was our second meeting with the heads of EMEA marketing. As we presented our solution to the room based on previous discussions about what they were looking for, I noticed the head of EMEA marketing had a deep frown appear across her forehead. It was only there for a second, just long enough for me to have noticed. I made a mental note to address it as soon as I had finished my sentence so she didn't forget her thought. It would give me the opportunity to adjust course and focus on what she wanted me to focus on if needed. I knew we had fully understood the issue we were solving, so it was either she didn't like the way I was presenting or it was something else. As soon as I could I asked her what the frown had meant. My question gave her space to share her thoughts about the project that she had never mentioned to anyone in her team before and opened the door to her to put a new issue on the table and discuss the trouble she and her team were having. The head of marketing had now opened up a whole new project to us which we previously had no knowledge of. She later told me that had I not asked her about the frown, she would not have discussed that problem because she was unaware that we had experience with the specific system she was discussing. She would have lost out on working with, in my opinion, the expert in this area and we would have missed out on a great project. If I had attached my own meaning to her frown I would have assumed she didn't like how I was presenting or that she thought the solution wasn't right.

When you ask people about what certain verbal or nonverbal things mean, ask from a place of real curiosity and not from a place of causing offence or that of defensiveness. From this place of curiosity you can uncover some very interesting insights.

If it had turned out that the client frowned because she didn't like the way I was presenting the content, I would have handed over to my MD to continue. You need to have rapport with someone to listen fully. If we are not in genuine rapport, it just blocks the communication. A block in communication means you will not be co-creating anything or being collaborative. Imagine using this same technique when communicating with your team. You may very well open up Pandora's box, unleashing things you really didn't even know were there. The reality is that what comes up highlights what's going on under the surface and may cause some ripples, but you are now armed with information you previously lacked. Using this you can find real solutions for

> *some real problems and stop papering over the cracks and*
> *hoping that everything works out.*

As you get better at listening to people and observing, you can start to become more aware of your own body language. What's going on for you as the other person speaks?

When people speak to you, your body will give off messages and signals, sometimes without your awareness. The next time someone speaks to you and it evokes something in you, some kind of emotional shift, be it negative or positive, take notice of it. How has your body responded to that internal shift and impacted your behaviour? This observation gives you the opportunity to know yourself better. What has the other person either bumped up against or shared with you that has caused you to change? Knowing this helps us see beyond our day-to-day task of existence and function. It is this skill that sets us apart from other animals. It will help you experience your own truth and authenticity. We often hide our authenticity because showing it either means being vulnerable or because it's easier wearing the mask of a 'people pleaser' to avoid conflict or offending someone. Once we learn to communicate authentically, we can allow ourselves to feel more compassion.

Just because you are the CEO/MD etc. it does not mean that you are always right and don't have more to learn. Often the best learning comes from a place of openness and a willingness to listen. When we speak we merely repeat what we already know. Everyone has something of value to say or add. Great ideas often come from the most unlikely places. You don't know who in your team has an idea or thought that could transform your business or when this great idea will pop up. When you listen, try to listen free of judgment. Dismissing someone's idea as 'crap' (even if it is way out there) will only serve to humiliate the person who is sharing the idea and put a lid on their creativity. This is also true for you so try not to pooh-pooh your own ideas.

A practice I recommend is journaling. Journaling is an unfiltered way of aggregating your thoughts and ideas. It allows for us to just jot things down without judgment, and remember there is no need to filter your thoughts, this is just for you and you can go back to edit, filter and sift through what you have noted down.

"Why, sometimes I've believed as many as six impossible things before breakfast."

(Said by the Queen in *Through the Looking Glass*)

Alice in Wonderland by Lewis Carroll

Write down your wonderful ideas and impossible things, and then take the time you need to sift through those impossible thoughts and pick out the ones that you can make possible, making you and the people who work for you successful.

Part of the function of this role of the leader is to help facilitate your team to be able to be the best they can be and create an environment where people really listen to one another. I read an article this morning about the impact of not having a purpose has on employees. Part of people feeling like their job has a purpose and your company is one worth investing their time into is for them to be heard and for their opinion and ideas to have worth. That being said, you are bound to come across someone who speaks so much they ramble on and on about their ideas that it can get tedious and hard to hold your concentration. Set boundaries and limits on time, for yourself and for others. The exercise on journaling is particularly useful for ramblers; it helps them to sift through their own thoughts and teach them how to filter effectively.

The brain has plasticity, it has the ability to create new pathways which ultimately help us form new habits. The more something is repeated and practised, the stronger the connections of these neural pathways become. The ease with which you can do this varies from person to person. When you are busy, which I am guessing is more often than not, it is so easy to slip into the old patterns we have already developed. Despite your best intentions, when the going gets tough and there are huge time constraints, it's easier to just go to the stored reactions in your memory bank, the reactions based on your past experiences, beliefs or prejudices, and go with that. Using the same behaviour as you have used in the past to deal with similar problems leaves you with the exact same results as the last time. If you can learn to identify when you are just running old patterns of behaviour, then you have the power and ability to reshape it.

It is when we are pushed the hardest that implementing the changes becomes challenging. Yet it is at this very time when changes should be implemented if you want a different outcome from what you have always had. Persevere with this way of communicating and being present with someone. People you work with, and for, can be frustrating, annoying and can drive you round the bend. Trust me, I empathise with that. I don't always like the people I work with, in fact

I will go so far as to say I don't always like people. Along with all of the things that drive you crazy, people are also interesting, wonderful and have something of value to say. Everyone has dreams, desires, friends, families, emotions and all that other good stuff that makes us human. It is this very reason I love people. When you can learn to listen to people with all your senses, and be self-aware in your communication, conversations can become generative; it flips the conversation from survival to joint exploration.

Claudia was one of my direct reports. I had just joined as her head of department; in my first one-to-one with Claudia, she cried. Her tears were mainly out of frustration, she put it down to the issues she was having that had never been addressed. Claudia was a very bright senior account director, she worked long hours and was very weighed down by the pressure of time and the sheer volume of work she was given. Claudia was often impatient and snappy with her account manager, Eileen.

Eileen was relatively new to the team, she was chatty and was very rigid about the time she came into work, took her lunch and left. I encourage people to work normal working hours. The things that Claudia should have been OK with were in fact grating her because Eileen was spending two or three hours a day just chatting, which drove Claudia to despair. I'd also scheduled in meetings with each of my direct reports' team members. When I met with Eileen, she also cried. She felt that Claudia was snappy with her and didn't take the time to explain clearly what needed to be done. Eileen often felt a bit dumped upon and unappreciated. They had both created such a terrible pattern of communicating with one another, neither had even bothered to work out how to communicate or even really ask to be heard. They had spent so long just bottling up all the things that bothered them instead of looking for a solution of how best to work with each other. They were behaving like threatened animals that would take every opportunity to attack one another.

It was very obvious that Eileen and Claudia didn't really get on as people. Claudia had worked for the agency for many years. She joined when the team was small and she'd become friends with pretty much everyone else that worked there. It was hard at first for her to get her head around the fact that she didn't have to be friends with everyone she worked with, she just had to be respectful and vice versa. Eileen and Claudia had to work out a way of communicating with one another that worked. As Eileen's line manager, Claudia wanted to take the responsibility of initiating the discussions that needed to happen. Claudia knew she would have to be willing to listen to and hear what Eileen had to say. Eileen was new to the agency and was not used to working in the way Claudia had become accustomed to and felt a little overwhelmed by it all.

The next few weeks saw a great improvement in the way that Claudia and Eileen communicated and worked together. Claudia took her time explaining clearly what she needed from Eileen and Eileen in turn responded well and worked efficiently. A month later Eileen resigned; over the course of the month the communication between these two had improved so much that Eileen felt comfortable enough to tell Claudia she had made a mistake. She needed to do something that was more in line with her personality, and working in an agency was not it. If someone in your team leaves, let it be because they have found somewhere that gives them career progression or because they have identified either on their own or with you that the role is not for them. If people are leaving your organisation because of communication problems and how people behave with one another, then get someone to help you take a long hard look at the issues and start to remedy them.

If, like Claudia, we can check our thoughts and realise our negative thoughts about someone impacts how we behave towards them, then we can change our behaviours, which in turn changes how we think and feel about someone or something.

Mastering the art of communicating better allows us to open up a whole new realm of possibilities, and helps us to prevent unnecessarily burning bridges.

- With whom could you do with improving your communication?

  _____

  _____

  _____

  _____

- What will you do differently to actively listen to the person/people you are with?

  _____

  _____

  _____

  _____

- What are your default settings? Can you begin to be aware when you start to slip back into the 'old' way of responding or listening?

  _____

  _____

  _____

  _____

- Take notice of what is happening for you internally when someone is speaking to you.

  _____

  _____

  _____

- How has actively listening changed the quality of information you now receive?

  _____

  _____

  _____

- How has actively listening changed the quality of the conversation?

  _____

  _____

  _____

- What 'impossible' things did you think today? (keep a journal of these thoughts)

  _____

  _____

  _____

Chapter 4:
Caring mindfulness

The truth is that to be more aware of the self, the other and the collective, you have to be able to manage your stress and state of mind. There are many mindfulness courses and free meditation classes. If you have the time you may wish to try one or two. The benefits of mindfulness and meditation have been proven by researchers at some very prestigious universities around the world. Meditation and mindfulness help improve interpersonal relationships. It is a shame that more organisations do not encourage active mindfulness and meditation at work. The Dalai Lama speaks of caring mindfulness, and how it can transform human connections.

I have a very strong belief in the transformative power of compassionate communication. Mindfulness and meditation are an important part of becoming a compassionate communicator. Running a successful business and making money allows you to do the things you want to do for yourself, your family, friends and hopefully the wider collective/community. Learn to bring caring mindfulness into the workplace, to teach others how to manage stress.

A work environment with lower stress levels leads to people who are able to focus on the things that really matter.

Here are a few key skills to help you on your way:

- Meditation

- Task-based mindfulness

- Expectation management

- Learning to let go

Meditation

Meditation begins in the brain. Similar in nature to hypnosis, it can induce a trance or trance-like state. This is a different state from that of being asleep or being alert. When we are awake and alert, our sympathetic nervous system is active. It is the sympathetic nervous system that helps us walk, talk and feel stress. When in a state of meditation our parasympathetic nervous system 'turns off' the sympathetic nervous system, this allows us to go into a deep state of rest and relaxation. Our nervous system controls our entire body and our emotions produced by our brains. Our nervous system is made up of two main parts: the central nervous system and the peripheral nervous system.

The central nervous system is made up of your brain and spinal cord and the peripheral nervous system is made up of the cranial nerves, spinal nerves and the autonomic nervous system. It is both these systems working in unison that keep us functioning and feeling.

It is our brain that is responsible for our intellect, memories, coordination, involuntary actions, perceptions of pain and pleasure, controls our hunger, thirst, reproductive behaviour, controls voluntary behaviours, learning, reasoning, personality, emotions, monitors blood, and all the other wonderful functions. The spinal cord passes messages between the brain and the rest of the body. Messages are carried around the body by an impressive network of nerves to and from the brain and spinal cord. The central and peripheral nervous system work together through conscious thought and automatic response.

The autonomic nervous system is that part of the peripheral nervous system that controls the activities of the internal organs without conscious thought. The autonomic nervous system can itself be considered in two parts: the sympathetic nervous system and the parasympathetic nervous system. They have the opposite effect on one another.

Organ in the body/ tissue	Effect of sympathetic stimulation	Effect of parasympathetic stimulation
Heart	Increases heart rate and stroke volume	Decreases heart rate and stroke volume
Blood vessels	Increases blood pressure	Decreases blood pressure
Lungs (bronchi, bronchioles and intercostals)	Dilation	Constriction
	Reacts to danger and is partly responsible for the effects felt by stress	Partly responsible for the effects felt when you are calm and tranquil

Our physical bodies are one of the most fascinating and complex machines. When we suffer from stress in our life, be it emotional or mental, the body responds. The immediate response to stress is tension in the muscles, our heartbeat speeds up, our breathing becomes shallow and fast, the blood pressure rises and we produce higher levels of cortisol in our bodies. Cortisol triggers the body's fight or flight response. There are long-term health implications for each of us if our cortisol levels remain high for long periods of time. High levels of cortisol in the blood is linked to issues like high cholesterol, high blood pressure, type 2 diabetes, short-term hair loss, sleep issues, depression, anxiety, and the list goes on.

In 1967, the psychiatrists Thomas Holmes and Richard Rahe examined the medical records of thousands of patients to determine if there was a link between stressful events and illness. Patients were asked to add up a list of 43 life events, based on an associated score. A positive correlation was found between the level of stress they were under and their illness. Life is stressful enough with the tasks we have to complete and the things we want to achieve. The way we relate to one another and communicate need not be an additional stress. In 1970, Richard Rahe carried out a study testing the reliability of the stress scale as a predictor of illness. The scale was used on 2,500 US sailors, who were asked to rate scores of life events over six months. Over the following six months, the health of each sailor was recorded. There was a direct correlation between stress scale scores (commonly known as the Holmes and Rahe scale) and illness. The scale was tested cross-culturally and findings supported the hypothesis of a link between our levels of stress and illness. Details of the Holmes and Rahe scale and various versions of it can be found online. It's an interesting stress test and indicates your percentage chance of illness or changes in your health.

While some stress in our lives is considered normal, excessive stress increases our chances of getting ill, which then has knock-on effects on other parts of our lives. Meditation can activate your parasympathetic nervous system and help you reduce the effects of the cortisol in your body. Meditation has been shown to reduce the heart rate and deepen breathing. It improves concentration, sleep and focus.

If you already meditate and have a good meditative practice in place, then feel free to skip the rest of this section as you will probably have techniques of your own to give yourself the gift of peace of mind.

I have run meditation workshops for the last 23 years. I started out in my parents' living room as a teenager, progressing to my university bedroom and to the London Canal Museum and at yoga centres around London. I've taught meditation to individuals from all walks of life: CEOs, train drivers, yoga teachers, hedge fund managers, accountants, sales people, students and some friends. When I talk to people about meditation, I listen with interest to the reasons people tell themselves and me as to why they cannot or will not meditate.

I wonder if you recognise any of these as one of your own reasons not to meditate:

- *I don't have time*

- *I can't sit on the floor*

- *My mind is too active*

- *I don't have the patience*

- *I can't concentrate*

- *I start but then I just start making lists in my head, so there is no point*

- *I don't believe in God*

- *I don't believe in that religion*

- *It's something that hippies/yogis do*

- *It's all just mumbo jumbo*

By meditating you are being kind to yourself. Meditating is a way of giving yourself the gift of peace of mind. I'm yet to meet anyone who doesn't want peace of mind. Often people think that they will have peace of mind once they have achieved............ (fill in the blank), or done such and such. While hitting goals is important, the peace of mind knowing that you have completed one goal is short lived. It will only be there until you have set the next goal. Leaders need to be able to lead a team to hit the next milestone. Often you are only as good as your next deal. The stress that comes with constantly chasing something should not go unchecked. If you ignore stress and the havoc it plays with your body, you will not be left with the health and wellbeing to even enjoy your success. Manage your cortisol levels and start giving yourself peace of mind through meditation. There are large financial players like Goldman Sachs and JP Morgan who hire people to teach meditation to their staff. Look out for signs of stress in your teams. Stress is a ticking time bomb and a major cause of burnout. Meditation will help you make head space to handle what's right in front of you and clear your head cluttered by a million thoughts at once.

Now let's deal with the issue of time, which actually is a big one. It is possibly the most common reason I hear for not meditating. There are only 24 hours in a day, in this time we try to fit in sleep, work, play, chores, family, exercise, and for those of us unfortunate enough to have to commute to and from work, the time it takes to travel. When I first started working, I used to struggle to find the 20 minutes to meditate. I did, however, manage to find time to watch crappy TV while eating dinner and not really paying attention to either. I could be in the middle of writing a proposal or working my way through a spreadsheet and distract myself by browsing the internet for hours looking at useless rubbish or do some other mindless activity.

Over the last 15 years the distractions have only become worse as we have quicker access to them, which just makes me feel compelled to flip from one link to another. Think of all the social media apps that you have downloaded on to your smartphone that connects you to all the people you know who are also using the same apps. Each time someone you know updates something or makes a comment, you get an alert on your phone, which causes a light to flash that actually won't go away until you have opened each one. Suppose you could ignore it, but the flashing light just annoys you, then there are the emails that make you feel compelled to constantly compose, check and reply to at all hours of the day and night, every day.

The reality is that you could ignore all of it for some time if you chose – the messages from clients, staff, stakeholders and suppliers. You could ignore the social media apps and uninstall them from your phone but you'd feel disconnected from the outside world and followers would have to wait, with baited breath, to read your next witty and oh so cleverly crafted 140 character tweet. What if you lose a deal or miss something really important? So you choose to spend your time connected to people who are scattered across time zones. Constantly being connected and available to your clients, for example, at all hours comes at the cost of having peace of mind and a good night's sleep. Sometimes this type of always-on connectivity comes at the cost of interpersonal relationships.

We allow our peace of mind to be taken away so often, in fact we give it away. Be kind to yourself. I am guessing that suggestion is bringing up some resistance. Not many people even know how to be kind to themselves; taking time to meditate and giving you the permission to meditate and turn it all down for a few moments is being kind.

The reality is you don't even need to meditate for 20 minutes a day to feel the benefits of meditation. All you need is ten slots of 10 seconds. Yes, that's right, all you need is 10 seconds of down time as often or as little as you want. I tend to do this every couple of hours, to help keep my head clutter free.

Recipe for 10 second meditation

The ingredients: You

Location:
- Anywhere except when operating heavy machinery or driving (or pretty much if you are doing anything else that for some reason may cause harm if you close your eyes for 10 seconds)
- Sitting, standing or lying down
- Ideally somewhere where no one will speak to you for 10 seconds and preferably quiet but this is not necessary. Some days you will be fine meditating on a busy packed commuter train and other days you just need a silent space. Do whatever works for you.

Method:
1: Close your eyes.
2: In your mind give your body permission to relax, especially those muscles or joints that are holding any tension, allow the tension to release with every exhalation.
3: Inhale deeply and exhale slowly, fill your lungs until you feel your abdomen expand and then exhale slowly - to the count of 1, 2, 3 (3x).
4: As you breathe, visualise your breath as it goes in and as it leaves your body. If it helps for you to attach colours to the in and out breath then do that, I usually visualise my in breath as light blue and my out breath as grey taking with it all my worry. Some people prefer to feel the in breath as cool and refreshing and the out breath as hot and sharp.

Notes:

Your focus for the 10 seconds will only be on your breath. So there is likely to not be enough time for other thoughts to interrupt too much. But if for any reason your mind won't quieten down then just acknowledge the thoughts that come in, let them go and bring your attention back to your breathing. You don't have to only stick to 10 seconds, you are free to push it to as long as you like. But for longer meditations I use a mantra (or word) that I repeat over and over to help me focus.

Meditation can really be done anywhere. I have a special spot in my home dedicated to meditation. I usually use this spot for longer meditations when I have time to sit for 20 minutes, which is usually about once or twice a week. I meditate every single day, even if it is only for a few moments, while I am sitting in the garden, or at my desk, or standing on the train, I meditate often to help me declutter my mind. If you can't sit cross-legged on the floor, then it really does not matter. Do whatever works for you. It is all about trial and error, if one way doesn't work then try another, you are bound to find something that works for you.

Some people choose to use a mantra, which can be a sacred word/phrase, the word peace or whatever other positive affirmation you wish to use. Using a mantra during meditation is to help keep the mind from wandering. The mantra is repeated over and over in a loop, so there is something else to focus on beyond the breath. If you are very visual then perhaps in your mind's eye you can imagine a calm body of water and keep your focus on how still and peaceful the water is.

It's hard for some people to calm their monkey mind. Our thoughts jump from one to the next like monkeys in a tree. A common misconception of meditation is that you have to control thoughts when you meditate. What if someone told you that you don't have to force your mind to be quiet? We can't control what thoughts pop into our heads. We can control how we react or don't react to that thought.

All you have to do when you meditate, whenever you notice your mind drifting off and starting to jump around from one thought to the next, is to bring your awareness back to your breathing. Meditation is about finding a moment of stillness, to allow you to be. If you are focusing on breathing and nothing more for 10 seconds, congratulations, you have completed your first 10-second meditation. There is nothing to wait for and there is nothing that needs your concentration. You only need be present, to let yourself gently bring your awareness to your breath.

In the East, meditation is seen as part of the culture. Tai Chi, Chi Gong and Yoga are forms of mindfulness meditation. Each focuses on the union between the breath and the movements and nothing more. In the West these practices have increased in their popularity and neuroscience has proven that the mind has plasticity and shown the benefits of meditation. The brain can create new neural pathways with practice. The more one practises meditating, the more the sense of wellbeing that person has. Meditation has been shown to improve concentration, cognition, productivity and increased work satisfaction.

"Man's mind, once stretched by a new idea, never regains its original dimensions."

Oliver Wendell Holmes

Task-based mindfulness

In simple terms it means to keep your focus on the task you are doing at any given time, free from any distractions. When was the last time you were doing something and were distracted by your thoughts? Hundreds of thoughts pop into your head to distract you so you paid little or no attention to the actual task you were completing at that very moment. Task-based mindfulness is similar to meditation in that it is about focusing your attention. In this case the focus of attention is through the use of all your senses on the specific task you are doing. It is so easy for us to get lost in thoughts of things that have happened, or playing scenarios out in our heads of things that have yet to happen and may never even happen. Once you train your mind to keep its attention on what you are doing, you give your brain the time to create new pathways to support this new found skill. That mental peace, even while completing a task, will be a familiar place to go to. I am suggesting that you can reset your default setting, if you choose to. You can always use self-hypnosis or free online recordings to help you to stay focused, or work with a hypnotherapist, there is a hypnosis recording that can be downloaded from my website www.compassionism.com (don't worry it's free).

I read an article not too long ago that stated we have about 70,000 thoughts a day. I don't know of any studies to prove or disprove this fact, but assume for a minute that we do have 70,000 thoughts in 24 hours. You've learnt already quite successfully, without any training or coaching, which thoughts to just let zoom through. The reason I know this to be true is that if you gave attention to every one of these thoughts each and every day you would be so exhausted and never get anything done. There are still a lot of thoughts left that you do actually spend time on, still thoughts competing for your attention. You can fine tune this natural ability to sift through and choose what to give attention to and meditation will help with that. It will aid thoughts to flow in and out with ease, draw attention back to the task at hand and increase the levels of satisfaction you feel in your work.

We are a funny lot; for so many people the sense of happiness is tied up so strongly in achievements and successes. We constantly seem to be chasing the elusive thing called happiness. You have probably heard someone tell you that they are happy when the weather is good, people whose state of mind is determined by some external factor to them. If you are one of those people then I hate to be the breaker of bad news: unless you decide to make a change in your life, then you will always be chasing *happy*. The reality is that happiness is not a destination or a factor that is dependent on some external factor. You can go away on holiday but if you are carrying misery, I can guarantee, your misery has followed you across the world. If we can be fully present and aware of the task we are doing and give it our full attention, we can maintain a state of mental peace. It means we are not living in some past story or playing out some non-existent future scenario but actually doing the thing we need to be doing with the attention it deserves. This goes for conversations with your team – be present and give people your undivided attention.

Manage expectations

Managing expectations isn't only about learning to say no. It is about learning to know what to say yes to and being clear on what you cannot or will not do. In my years as a sales person I have come across all sorts of people in business, those that overpromise and underdeliver (never a good thing) and those who underpromise and overdeliver. I don't know many employees or clients who feel disappointed with the outcome of projects where expectations have been managed from the start, when everyone is in agreement with the outcome and time frames. Managing expectations can be the difference between client/ employee satisfaction or disappointment. When people are disappointed you are likely to get an earful, lose some of your income, you risk setting yourself up for a loss of reputation, and your reputation in an oversaturated market is all you have to rely on.

For a moment consider the following: you have 100 people's salaries to pay, the rent is due, several clients have yet to pay, one of your largest clients has reduced the spend with you, with no prior notice. You have agreed to take on some work for a new company and you have oversold yourself because you want to win the logo. They have given you an unrealistic deadline for the work to be delivered and the brief is almost non-existent. Under pressure you have agreed to do this – after all, you have pulled it out of the bag before. You take this back to the team and you turn up the heat, you hand over the work expecting them to deliver. To throw a spanner in the works, you let the team know they have to work with a third party, which you need to rely on to get things to you. After throwing this at them, you step away.

I can tell you that being on the receiving end of that is no party. Yes occasionally, it is great to have a project come along that seems impossible and have the satisfaction of getting it done well. This is only acceptable if this behaviour and the pressure cooker environment this creates is the exception not the norm. It is vital that you manage the workload for yourself and your employees. Working ridiculously long hours each and every day under such pressure is not sustainable.

Sally dedicated her entire young adult life to her work, she was the woman who would come into work before everyone else and leave really late at night. She would stop for a quick 'lunch break' at her desk and then grab a pizza and a bottle of wine on her way home after 10.30pm. She did make a lot of money, and moved up the corporate career ladder. Everyone wanted her on their team. Not once did anyone stop and think of the cost of working like this on her. Sally has a work ethic that all employers wish every one of their employees had: she was hardworking, straight talking and went beyond the call of duty. Sally burnt both ends of the candle; after working 14-16 hours, she would go out drinking with friends until late or get through a bottle of wine by herself in her flat before going to bed. She said it helped her switch off from the stress of her day. She would often stay up watching TV and work until 2am. She'd still come into work really early the next day. She had little to no time for a relationship or hobbies. She lived in an expensive London neighbourhood, yet by her own admission she wasn't enjoying her life because she dedicated the majority of her 24 hours to work.

Shortly after her 45th birthday she fell very ill which left her unable to work. It was only then that she began to change things because she realised that working so hard hadn't given her what she needed from her life, so she took up art classes, went to the gym and began dating. She always wanted children and a partner, but for the last 25 years she didn't make time or have the space in her life for it, because work took over.

As an employer you are not responsible for how someone like Sally chooses to spend their time. You do, however, have a moral duty as a human to at least manage the number of hours people dedicate of their time. If you do not look after the goose that lays your golden egg, and don't ensure it gets the correct amount of time to eat, stretch and rest, it will only get sick and stop producing golden eggs for you to sell. As I said before, I do not believe there is such a thing as work/life balance, it is all simply life. How will you choose to help your teams learn to manage and maximise their time? How will you choose to spend your own time?

Working long hours with no breaks and expecting great results is absurd. When the people in my team regularly couldn't seem to get their work done within their contracted working hours, I began wondering if they needed time management training or if I needed to help them reallocate work to other members of the team. Had I miscalculated workloads and what was realistically achievable each day? Did I need to look at getting in a temp or simply hire more people? Working really long hours ought to be the exception and not the norm. I didn't want my golden geese to choke. However, when needs must, you and your team need to be willing to roll up their sleeves and muck in.

I had a particularly demanding client who would email at 4am GMT, and expect to get an instant reply. The client and I were in different time zones which didn't necessarily help. He was based in Denver, USA and I was in London, UK. If he had to wait more than an hour for me to reply, he would email the MD and tell him that I wasn't doing my job. Luckily for me the MD knew I would handle it and left it to me to deal with. This client was really not used to anyone saying no to him, or managing his expectations, because he was used to getting his way from his suppliers. The trouble is that he had always worked with agencies that were willing to pull their pants down at every command. It was not how I wanted to work and if he wanted to work with an account director who put solving clients' problems as the highest priority, then I was the woman for the job. I knew we would have to come to some kind of mutually respectful way of working. So I picked up the phone and addressed his concerns. I let him know that I would offer him the best solution and fix his issues and get things done right. He in return had to respect that I would not be answering emails at 4am. I had a rule that I did not check work emails between the times of 8pm and 8am unless there was an exceptionally urgent deadline. I did ask him to think about it, and if he didn't like that, then I would happily find him a different account director to work with. Needless to say, he was not used to having his expectations managed and he respected what I had said and agreed for us to work this way. After that point he didn't ever email the MD again to complain. It all worked out just fine, he didn't give me the hard time he gave to everyone else and we built a great working relationship.

If you don't respect your time then no one else will. Unless you are a medical professional that saves lives, put things in perspective. We simply work at helping people make more money, get promoted and look good to their bosses, in the process, of course, making money ourselves. If a client emails you at 5pm on a Friday expecting someone to be able to make some major changes to some online advertising, which will take at the very least eight hours and expects it back in 30 minutes, unless you have infinite resources sitting around doing nothing to be able to throw at it, at that very moment, the client's expectations have to be managed. You have to let people know when the work can be done by. It is not worth you throwing your staff to the wolves. Yes, you have to do what is right by the client; after all, you have to earn a living and have to keep them happy. There does also need to be some balance, because taking advantage of your employees is not the best way.

It was strange to me that one of my bosses would often ask me at 8am, "Did you see the email I sent you last night?" (which would have been sent to me at midnight). "I haven't got a reply from you yet." Having just about managed to get some sleep, get showered and get to work, and I'm expected to reply already, surely that was a trick question? There are only a few things you ought to be doing at midnight; sending or reading work emails is not one of them. Put and keep things in perspective.

Learning to let go, keeping things in perspective

It is important that we learn or get help to let things go. When you don't let things from the past go, the only person you are really harming is yourself. You keep yourself imprisoned with memories or injustices that have been done to you. To really let go involves forgiveness. Forgiving yourself or the other person(s) involved.

If letting go is a hard thing for you to do or the hurts are so deep rooted, then perhaps practise with letting go of the small things first. This will help make day-to-day life that much easier. If someone cut in front of you this morning while you were on your way to work and you got annoyed about it, if you allow that annoyance to build up inside you and anger towards them to grow, the only person that is being beaten up is you. It hasn't bothered the other person at all. You have allowed the feelings of annoyance to trickle into your behaviour that day. Developing a regular meditative practice will help you let things go and keep things in perspective. It helps us build our resilience. Why have you let someone else's idiotic actions impact your day? It may have thrown you off course for a second, which is probably fairly normal. It is how quickly you can recover from that which is most important. We don't often look at things from someone else's point of view. Perhaps they had to get to a really important interview, or had to rush someone to the hospital, or maybe they are just an impatient jerk. Don't let someone else's actions be the blame for how you are feeling as their behaviour was not about you.

A wise person once told me that if you are pointing the finger at someone else and blaming them for something, there are three fingers pointing right back at you. You have the ability to put things into perspective and control how you feel. Sometimes I just don't want to put things into perspective and want to have a rant and rave and be a moody so-and-so. I do this with the conscious knowledge that I am giving myself permission to behave this way. My dear friend Anna once told me in the middle of a rant I was having, "Don't you think you are overreacting slightly?" I hated hearing that, and didn't like her for saying it. That was many years ago now, and from that day, each time I have a rant or let someone else affect my day I hear her asking me that question. I have a huff about it and am usually in denial about such behaviour, but it helps me let things go. What is it that you carry around and replay in your head that you drag around with you like a big heavy suitcase everywhere you go. It's exhausting dragging your stuff everywhere you go.

I know I need to let go of even more hurt from my life and the injustices I have experienced. When my own suitcase pops its lid open, spilling its contents into my life, I still sometimes allow it to impact my behaviour. When it does, I revert to my meditative practice and realise I cannot change the past and will not allow my future be enslaved by it. What thoughts or experiences or events in your life do you allow to control you? Build your resilience to let things go, forgive yourself and others, so you make space in your head and heart.

- Have you measured your stress levels?

  _____

  _____

  _____

  _____

- In what areas of your life could you use more mindfulness?

  _____

  _____

  _____

  _____

- What have you experienced after a week of meditating?

  _____

  _____

  _____

- What situations need expectation management?

  _____

  _____

  _____

- How can you manage expectations better?

  _____

  _____

  _____

  _____

- What is holding you back?

  _____

  _____

  _____

  _____

- What could you do with letting go of?

  _____

  _____

  _____

- What do you need to put into perspective?

  _____

  _____

  _____

Chapter 5:
Create a culture of compassion

If you explore the company culture of a small to medium-sized organisation that is doing really well and keeps growing, you will notice that when it comes to their staff they are:

- **L**earning environments – this aids innovation and personal growth

- **I**nclusive – this encourages teamwork

- **C**ollaborative – this encourages discussion and creativity

- **G**enerative – this helps individuals come together to see different perspectives and create new options that previously didn't exist

- **E**mpowering

You may have heard of a young gentleman in the USA, Dan Price, who is the CEO of credit card payment processing firm Gravity Payments. This young entrepreneur made the decision that he will pay his staff a minimum wage of $70,000 (approximately £45,000) a year. It was a bold move, it was his way of making a statement to the people who work for him: *"I value you and I think you deserve a bigger share of the profits."* This bold step caused a lot of controversy and ruffled a few feathers. His socialist move did not go down well in the corporate American capitalist culture which does not support it. Basic wages need to be at a level that people can afford to live and not have to struggle to buy food or pay rent. Dan's decision in 2014 was a brave thing to do. The consequence of that decision is that he now has to rent out his home to make ends meet. Your altruism and desire to create a culture that you can be proud of should be something that is sustainable. One step at a time, I know our world needs radical changes and some major shifts. Change has to be managed well, starting with the things you can change and implement that are sustainable and self-generating.

Many MDs/ CEOs I have worked with believe that their organisation is inclusive and everyone is part of 'one big happy family'. Families by their very nature are dysfunctional, as we become part of situations that stop us from speaking from a place of authenticity and inability to communicate with one another well. There are, however, families who function better than others and are happier than others, because they have learnt how to communicate with one another in a more authentic and caring manner. Their communication style keeps in mind the greater good of the collective.

Individuals are usually only included within a group/team if they have a shared vision, the same values and a commitment to a common goal. Business leaders are often so far removed from the day-to-day interactions and communications between people that they just see what they want to see and do not really notice underlying issues. Creating a business culture that you can be proud of and leave as your legacy begins by paying attention to the way in which people communicate, what they say and how they say it. There are definitely things you can do to get things on track and get your organisation to a place where it is one functional team who know how to communicate with compassion.

A thriving family share core values by living by them on a daily basis. Sometimes we don't even have a conscious awareness that something is a value until someone bumps up against that value. I hold kindness as a core value; when people behave in a way that is unkind towards another human, I am reminded of my value, and those feelings are really strong. We all come to a work environment having very different sets of core values, and will no doubt bump up against other people's values.

Uniting people to a shared value is important. The only way to really get people to buy into the company values is by embodying those values. Values are not something that you can preach; they are things that we begin to accept as part of who we are. Bring your team together with a collective value that you all share in your work, towards a collective goal. You might have honesty as a value for your company, but if you allow dishonesty within your organisation then how can your staff hold honesty as a value to your customers? Look after your staff and the customers will be taken care of.

Being heard is a fundamental part of being included, knowing that your voice matters. I have already covered some of this in Chapter 3, it is important so worth revisiting. When you take time to listen to people, stay away from any judgment and do not allow your prejudices to get in the way, you allow a space for a deeper meaningful connection to another human. People want to be heard, without feeling like they are being judged. People share ideas and knowledge by communicating. Trying not to defend your ideas over and above other people's can be hard.

A professor at MIT, Otto Schemer, delivers a course on the transformation of society and business and he uses a great analogy of how to disassociate from one's ideas. Imagine your idea is a jacket. Disassociating yourself from ownership of your idea is like taking off a jacket. I wear the jacket so thus the jacket is mine, I am wearing it. As soon as you take the jacket off, it is simply that, just a jacket. The same goes for ideas: as soon as you are able to be open to sharing and accepting ideas without being so connected to your own ideas is when real collaboration and co-creation happens. If you allow people to speak and the space to share ideas, you let them know that their voice matters. People's voices being heard can change lives.

Malala Yousafzai is the youngest person to be awarded a Nobel peace prize. Imagine what would have happened if no one allowed her to share her voice, and take a stand for the basic rights of young girls to get an education. Knowing your voice matters, and for others to hear your voice and truth, can change hearts and minds. Not everyone is Malala, we are not fighting that kind of battle or injustice. You certainly have ideas, some useful and some not so much. Just give the voice and content a space to live and breathe and sift through what is useful. You never know what you can create.

When people feel heard, they feel valued; knowing this will aid you in facilitating your team to work towards a common goal. Give your staff a purpose to their work, give people measurable and realistic targets. Don't set people up for failure, you want your business to excel and be the best. Each time someone in your team hits a target, no matter how small, celebrate it. Celebrate each small victory and be proud of one another. In my family, we celebrate everything. Any excuse to have a mini impromptu party. There'd be a mini party if any of us passed a piano exam. When I completed my first on-stage dance performance in front of 2,000 people we had a party. There'd be cause to celebrate and we celebrated each completion and milestone. It added an element of fun to completing tasks/goals. In retrospect it was much more than that – it was our mini victories that saw us through the tough times. Every family has their share of drama and issues.

I know people whose families didn't really celebrate anything. When my friend Jay got 98% in an exam, instead of celebrating their child's success, the child would be asked what happened to the other 2%. People whose achievements were never celebrated have a tendency to be hard on themselves and everyone around them. Start by cultivating a habit of feeling gratitude. The more you begin to be grateful for the wondrous things in your life, of which your business is a part, you will notice more good stuff to be grateful for, and the happier you will be. No matter what habits you learnt from your family while growing up, if you want to see more compassion in your organisation, then start with celebrating people's achievements along the way. This will help people weather the storms with you, it creates a sense of solidarity.

When we have to have a difficult conversation with someone, it can leave us feeling a bit anxious. The solution, to ease the anxiety for both of you, is to have a generative discussion; just flip the conversation from being about individual survival to joint exploration. Find a solution to the issues you have to deal with together and be prepared for some defensiveness. Not everyone is willing to take responsibility for finding a solution to a problem, regardless of whether they were or were not part of creating it. In coaching terms, this joint exploration is to create a new paradigm that didn't previously exist. Our minds are incredibly generative; we produce and create things all the time. I'm an advocate of generative conversations as this type of communication is free from attack and defence. It is about laying out the facts, like pieces of a jigsaw, in front of you, and taking a step back. It gives you a chance to observe and take in the new information, to look at it from different perspectives and create something new together with what's been put on the table.

My university degree is in sciences; science is based on proving or disproving an hypothesis through experimentation. It is all about trial and error, based on factual information. I see life as no different. We try things and if they don't work we try something else until we find a way of doing something that does work. We know that communicating with other human beings with compassion and keeping the other in mind when we speak takes the sting out of difficult conversations. We can then give space for something new to form (this space would have previously been filled with attack and defence) so that everyone leaves feeling like they put in the necessary effort to create something new. It is in business that I feel this formula for communication is used the least but where it is needed the most. The truth is we have to stop being arseholes to one another.

Compassionate communication helps us create a space for honesty. Honesty that isn't a personal attack but a respectful expression of what is going on for each of us, in order to work through the issues and then let them go. Compassionate communication in an organisation also means not allowing a culture of talking about someone behind their back. I'm embarrassed to even admit I have done this myself at work. If you are guilty of doing this then stop it. As a business leader, it is up to you to set the example and tone that is used in your company. It is only with honesty and respect that you will create a team. A cohesive team trust one another and will 'have each other's back' and not throw each other under a bus at any given opportunity. As a business leader, it is important to surround yourself with people that will be straight with you, who tell you the truth and also with that truth be willing to offer a solution. If you as a leader can learn to listen to that truth and be honest with your staff with a pinch of kindness and compassion, you are showing your staff that you respect them and value the input they have to give you and the business.

First start with your leadership team, the people who will help facilitate this space for the rest of the employees in your business. Make your senior leadership team a priority and for them to see the senior leadership team goals as a priority. It is hard for people who have different roles within an organisation to come together and see each other as a team.

The sales director's priority and first team is often the sales team, the marketing director's priority is the marketing team, the IT director's priority is the IT team and the same goes for finance, operations, production and so on. Each of these job roles requires a very different skill-set and very different personality types. As a business leader, your responsibility is to bring these heads of departments together and facilitate open, honest and generative dialogue. It is vital for these heads of departments to come together as a team. Your strength as a leader will come from this core team, as they will be the ones to help take your business to the next level.

Creating a culture that you and others can be proud of is not something that can be done alone. You need your core team on board if you want to achieve this to become a productive, efficient, creative organisation.

Creative organisations are innovative ones and innovative organisations give individuals the space to experiment and make mistakes. Innovation can only happen when people have a clear mind to help the process. Greatness takes time, patience and consistent nurturing. Google didn't become the organisation it is today by squashing experimentation. They encouraged people to explore through experimentation. Their greatness comes from sharing ideas and giving space for greatness to grow. Once you empower your teams to make decisions you give them the power to create. This creativity leads to product/service development and your staff going the extra mile. Make it safe for individuals within your organisation to do crazy out of the box things, by reducing personal risk and embracing a sense of collective risk.

I once worked for an organisation where the VP held so tightly to the business that it suffocated the people and disempowered them. This disempowerment leads to paralysis, an inability to progress and fulfil one's potential. If you think people are not trustworthy and can't do the job, why hire them and keep them? Let them go and work for someone else who will give them the space and empowerment to reach their highest potential. This disempowerment can lead to people being 'beaten into submission' and they will simply perform as robots, doing what they are told and programmed to do. They will be afraid to use their own power of judgment, to collaborate with clients to come up with solutions. They will be constantly worried that their judgment is wrong and they will be reprimanded if they don't do exactly as instructed. And not doing exactly as you say could cost them their job and the wrath of your aggression, passive or active. You are seen as a threat to their financial security, which combined with your aggression leaves them in a constant state of high alert and stress. Nothing good can come of decisions made when we are stressed. Leave your inner control freak at home. Give your staff the freedom to fulfil the role they have been hired for. Killing the golden goose isn't the answer.

Some time ago I was hired by a creative agency as head of a key account. The thing that surprised me the most is that no one at this organisation had met with the client's EMEA VP of Marketing. When I heard this, I remember thinking why the hell not? Surely getting to know their goals, drivers and priorities first-hand was important. Rather than hearing the regurgitated version from his team, who all had their own personal agenda, the CEO and MD that I worked for

> *would not allow me to reach out and set up a meeting with the VP of EMEA Marketing of the account. I was meant to be heading up this account and there was a reluctance to relinquish control. There was such a hierarchical culture of fear and control at this agency that it was hindering my team and me from fulfilling our role properly.*

If you want any job done well, allowing people to connect with one another to get different perspectives and information is part of that process. Facilitating and supporting these things within your organisation will help create new avenues of income. More income = more profit. Encourage collaboration between your teams, clients and suppliers to share ideas and listen actively and celebrate the collective wins. Even Thomas Edison didn't invent the light bulb alone, he too had help. We just don't hear about those people like Humphrey Davy and Joseph Swan. You didn't get to where you are alone. Even your wins involved other people, in some way, shape or form – for example the client who gave you your first opportunity to show them what you are capable of.

> *I had a colleague who had a real superiority complex and never acknowledged that anyone else was ever involved in her success. Let's call her Samantha. Samantha and I used to work at an integrated demand generation organisation, we sold call centre and email services. Nothing particularly glamorous, but we both did a really good job. Samantha and I were very different in approach to work. I used to take the time to go and speak to the telemarketers who worked on*

my client campaigns to find out who exactly was working on the campaign, and if the client asked me about the team, I knew first-hand how things were going. I enjoyed getting to know the people who were allowing me to get more business and be successful. I owed each successful business close not just to my ability to sell and close a deal, I also owed it to the callers. They worked hard all day, for a fairly basic wage, on the phone generating leads for my clients. It was this that allowed me to be successful. Every six months there would be a party for the callers held by the operations teams and they would invite the sales team. I bumped into Samantha in the lift on my way down to the call centre to go and celebrate their hard work with them and assumed Samantha was coming along too. I asked if that's where she was heading, her response struck me as the most absurd thing to say, "I'm not socialising with them!" Just to clarify, I asked if she felt they were beneath her. To which she responded of course they were. It was a very egocentric and arrogant view of the world.

To Samantha these people held no value as people, they were merely a replaceable resource. I can honestly say that no matter how good you are as a sales person, if your product is no good then I assure you that your revenue stream will dry up. You won't be taking home your nice shiny commission cheque next month. It was the skills and dedication of the callers allowing me to sell with conviction and belief. Each time a new project would go to the calling floor the callers would ask whose project it was. Their preference would always be to work on the projects I had brought in over the ones Samantha had brought in. I didn't understand, before this encounter with Samantha, as to why. It was through this that I got the best callers, the best results and closed all of the larger new business deals. I had got to know them and treated each of them with integrity.

One valuable lesson to keep in mind is that it doesn't matter if someone is the cleaner or the CEO, they are both human. They both matter and both deserve your respect.

In most businesses it is the sales people who have the biggest egos and they are also typically your most expensive employees. They are the ones who get kudos for closing big deals, even with existing clients, the production or operations teams also deserve a pat on the back too. It is their hard work that helped facilitate this win. Showing humility, thanking and acknowledging others' contributions to your success, encourages team work and collaboration.

I have mentioned previously one of Newton's laws of physics states that energy cannot be created or destroyed, it can only change from one form to another. Have you noticed the energy differences you feel in the air around you when you walk into a situation that is tense and stressful vs. walking into a room full of people who are happy and joyous, relaxed and calm? If you have never noticed these differences before, I invite you to experiment and become the observer. In NLP terms this energy is called the field. It is the energy field created and held by a group of people. There is also the wider field which is the energy held by people in a specific country or region or the energy field across a continent and our world. I am not talking about gravity, what I am referring to is the energy we share between us. We unconsciously respond to this field.

There are exercises for you to use, to start becoming aware of the field and the impact it has on those around you. If it helps to get someone on board to help you with this exercise, do so. It's very interesting to watch what comes of it. Try by first creating a generative space that allows for honesty and creativity. If this is so far removed from the norm within your organisation then you may have everyone in the room look at you with suspicion and distrust, in which case I suggest you start implementing the first few ideas in this book first and make internal changes. The field in NLP can also be described as our collective consciousness.

- What is it that we are all aware of that is going on in our collective energy and thoughts?

- What is it in our collective energy that wants to help create a future that allows for you to help other people be successful, as well as give attention and focus to your own success?

We can achieve much more collectively than we can on our own. It took hundreds and thousands of craftsmen to build the Seven Wonders of the World and help bring one person's idea/vision to life. Alone we cannot do anything, together we can create such incredible things. Having trust and giving permission to oneself and others to explore what might be possible together to build something fantastic. Google creates a culture of honesty, the heads of the business share all their innovative ideas with their staff. They trust them with 'secret' strategy and product plans. If the trust is broken, which it has been in the past, people are let go. Trust and honesty is risky, but incredibly rewarding, as people get on board to make these plans successful. Even Richard Branson didn't become a business icon by himself. He surrounded himself with the right people who helped hold the field for creativity. The fact he is slightly eccentric and willing to take risks certainly helps.

My parting words of wisdom to my old team were, if you want to climb up the corporate ladder and be successful in your career, make sure you help other people be successful and achieve their best potential: the energy this creates supports creativity, collaboration and innovation. Create a culture that you and your team can be proud of, a culture that can outshine and outperform any other. Not by badmouthing the competition or stealing business, but purely by being better than you were yesterday. Give individuals the permission to do something extraordinary in a risk-adverse culture.

- What is the culture of your organisation?

  _____

  _____

  _____

- What would you like it to be?

  _____

  _____

- What in your work and life are you grateful for?

  _____

  _____

- What will be the next achievement that will be celebrated?

  _____

  _____

- What was the most recent achievement in your team that you will celebrate?

  _____

  _____

- What can you do to encourage more creativity within your team?

  _____

  _____

  _____

- Where are you willing to allocate some decision-making power?

  _____

  _____

  _____

- What are you willing to risk for success?

  _____

  _____

  _____

- Where can you be more transparent with your team?

  _____

  _____

  _____

  _____

Chapter 6:
People make business successful

The most profitable and successful companies invest in their people. I was at a training seminar for a couple of days at a hotel just outside London and at breakfast happened to sit next to and have a discussion with a PWC graduate employee. I learnt that PWC, for example, send their graduate recruits on residential induction training courses. This is after they have gone through the already rigorous recruitment process to get the job in the first place. This type of intensive immersive training serves three main purposes.

1: It helps the organisation communicate the values and ethos of the company. Once the graduates really understand these values, they are put in front of clients. They are given the knowledge they need to get started. They know what is expected of them and the boundaries have been set. Creating alignment between the organisation and individuals' expectations.

2: This type of residential training lets the graduates know that they are valued: 'we (the organisation) commit to and invest in your development and empowerment', which in turn generates loyalty and commitment. These young minds will invest in the business that hires them, as the heads of the business invest in their career progression, development and growth. This type of programme is of significant benefit to the bottom line.

3: To get these young recruits to build lasting bonds with one another, generate a sense of camaraderie and develop healthy competition. This is fantastic because it frees you up to not have to 'baby-sit'. These bonds mean that they will be each other's motivators and develop a self-managing support system. It empowers the graduates to use their collective consciousness.

Like any training programme, the learning needs to be topped up and reinforced for it to be compounded, or all the money spent on this would have been for nothing as all the learning gets lost.

The best educational establishments in the world will not just want the child with the best grades but also the child who is the 'all-rounder' who pushes past the comfort zone and tries a number of other things and has developed different skills. The best workplaces also recruit with similar criteria. The people that these businesses recruit are happy to try new projects. They have the ability to switch from right brain to left brain if and when needed. These are the kind of people who can roll up their sleeves and get stuck into numerous different tasks and projects and accomplish each one well. Can you imagine a technical engineer writing a book on mindfulness and meditation?

Google is an example of an organisation in the tech space where individuals would love to work and be a part of. We all know that Google famously has nap pods in the office and gives free breakfasts, lunches and dinners to staff. Studies show the huge benefits of rest and taking naps on the function and alertness of the brain. We are not in the industrial age anymore, the hours we work and how we work can be as flexible as we allow. If the brain is alert it's going to be more creative and productive than an exhausted one. We don't need any studies to tell us that.

Google also very famously gives its employees 20% of their working hours to create something based on their personal passions that will help the company. A Google engineer, Chade-Meng Tan, wrote a book on meditation and mindfulness. By allowing this, Google encourages employees to be creative and step out of their box and comfort zone and challenge themselves and it extends one's knowledge base. The 80:20 rule they apply is of huge benefit to Google. Google is, after all, a business, but unlike many organisations it's a business that really cares about its employees and the employees' families. You only have to read their death in service policy to know just how much compassion they show. Google pays the deceased's spouse or domestic partner 50% of their salary for 10 years and each child of the employee receives US$1,000 (£705) per month until they turn 19 or 23 (for full-time students). While employee benefit programmes like the ones Google has can improve retention, and may appear to improve performance, these types of perks are a step in the right direction towards a more socially conscious business.

The reason I use Google as an example is not to suggest that you go and have nap pods installed or that you give 20% of your IT helpdesk guys' time to teaching yoga. It is to show you the value of creativity simply by cultivating an environment that allows flexibility. If the Google model of flexibility is a step too far, then start with the simplest thing to be flexible with your employees' time. If the hours you contract people to work for you is eight, let's say they typically work on average those eight hours. A few nights/weeks in a row they have been in the office until way after the cleaners have been and gone. Then they should be given the flexibility to come in 30 minutes late one day when there is nothing urgent happening that morning, or for them to leave a little early one Friday.

Be flexible with your staff and they will reward you with their hard work and loyalty, because they feel you care about their wellbeing. When people give you more hours than you pay them for, and thus more work than what would realistically be possible in those eight hours, acknowledging that and not taking advantage of it is the compassionate thing to do. If someone needs to leave to go to the doctor or has a sick child and needs to rush off early, or simply has a flight to catch, let them have the time and make up the hours when it is really busy and you need the extra hands on deck. They will be happier and will freely give it to you.

There are a number of great organisations who have the ethos of people first, profits second. They are the socially conscious organisations that I call the Jiminy Crickets of the business world. They are the people who run businesses that are dripping with humanity. They are ethical, moral and want to better our world. A good example of this is Ben &

Jerry's, who source their half-baked brownies from a social enterprise, Greystone Bakery. This bakery provides jobs and job training for individuals who face difficulties in getting mainstream employment. Greystone Bakery has an open door hiring policy: anyone that goes through their front door is given the opportunity to work if they want it. Regardless of their past, be it having been in prison, homelessness or previous drug and alcohol abuse, when a job becomes available, the next person on the waiting list is given a job, no questions asked. Could Ben & Jerry's do without the brownies from this bakery? There may very well be a cheaper alternative yet they choose to be socially responsible and give back to society.

The cosmetic company Lush in the UK uses aprons made through a social enterprise called Re-wrap, who support underprivileged women in India – not because these aprons are the cheapest option but because it is the right thing to do. In addition to making cruelty-free products, they have another great opportunity to give back to the world.

Every change starts with a single step. As a business leader, it is your responsibility to know that the business you intend doing is good business. Not all business is good business, and if you want to be a leader who earns the respect of your teams then you must be willing to stick by your principles and not drop your pants for the sake of a business deal. One of my mentors once told me that if you are going to stick to your principles, then you have to be willing to lose out on something.

Early in my career I worked for the technology division of a consulting firm. A Far Eastern telecommunications company (let's call them ETC) was hosting an event in the Middle East and wanted our lead telecommunications analyst to attend as one of the keynote speakers. This analyst, Pritesh, is Indian; he studied at a very well-established and reputable university in the UK. He earned a first-class honours degree and masters in Telecommunications. ETC had asked for our leader in the field to be the keynote speaker. Pritesh has an incredible education, is very articulate, intelligent and witty. Upon learning that Pritesh was Indian, ETC's head of communications decided that they did not want him to be the keynote speaker. ETC asked if there was someone else we could send in his place that was Caucasian. This person had to deliver the talk intelligently and answer questions on the research that Pritesh had done. The correct response from the company I worked for would have been something along the lines of 'thank you for asking us to be part of your event but we think you should find someone else, we do not condone such racism and prejudice'. Instead the head of UK operations suggested that our head of department went to the event in Pritesh's place. Our head of department was an incredibly intelligent woman, she was Caucasian and at least met that criteria. Still not satisfied with the outcome, ETC then came back once more and said no, we want a Caucasian male to deliver this keynote speech.

This was the second opportunity the organisation I worked for had to say no to working with this company, this time also on grounds of sexism. Still NO! The company dropped their principles, all for the sake of a few thousand pounds.

> *From that instant the company lost a significant amount of respect from its employees. In the end the then technical sales director, who really knew nothing of the content and had very little cultural sensitivity, went to the Middle East to deliver a keynote speech to a group of telecommunications engineers and ETC's potential clients. Needless to say, they were not impressed with their investment (not a surprise) and did not spend any money on the research the company was banking on for them to do.*

If you ever find yourself in a situation similar to this, don't compromise your principles or reputation. Even Transport for London and the NHS don't stand for any verbal abuse towards their staff. So why would you stand for this kind of blatant racism and sexism in the 21st century? We live and work in a multicultural society. If potential clients don't like it and you employ people of multiple ethnicities, then you need to be respectful to them first and tell the client to go elsewhere. There are huge benefits to you and your organisation in making sure that your staff are looked after. Holding your principles earns you respect and living and breathing your business values leads by example – what I like to refer to as a compassionate business. Businesses exist to make money and be profitable. The world does not need any more businesses that are profitable at the cost of humanity. It is this type of selfish business that has created the inequality and problems that we have to solve in the world.

Ben & Jerry's know that by investing in helping people make a living and caring for the community they too get great press coverage and there is a real feel-good factor in buying Ben &

Jerry's ice cream. I am knowingly contributing to the profits of such a great organisation (and my growing bottom). The truth is that running a business that has the employees and the wellbeing of people at the core of its values leads to an increase in ROI. Consider this:

Reduction in stress ➔ increase in creativity ➔ decrease in staff turnover ➔ decrease in sick days ➔ Increased productivity ➔ increased motivation ➔ increased commitment ➔ increase in loyalty ➔ more money

Once you and your leadership team learn to really communicate with compassion, it opens an avenue for dialogue and collaboratively focuses on solutions to issues. Wouldn't it be great to resolve issues with ease? Communicating with compassion will give you all the permission to have time to think, to be able to go away and sleep on a decision and you can then return to discuss possible solutions together on how to get things moving and flowing again. The long-term benefits to your business will be huge. I am not saying there won't be some people who will never want to change or evolve, there will always be those people. Overall, if you can invest in your people, the majority will respond well, and if they feel looked after, your clients will also be looked after as your staff will be more than happy to go the extra mile.

The age-old sales saying that *people buy from people* applies within the confines of your business too. People will not necessarily remember what you did or said, they will remember how you made them feel. If you undermine or undervalue your staff and choose not to apologise when you have done wrong by them, your staff will underperform and your clients suffer as a result of it. Your staff will become resentful and disengage; at worst they will sabotage you. You can hope they will find a new job and leave, but if they don't you are stuck paying someone who really doesn't want to be there and you have done nothing to improve the situation. Two of the most important aspects of the concept *people buy from people* are:

1. **To listen and be present with all your senses**

    Allow yourself to really be with someone and work out collaboratively what can be done about a difficult situation you are facing with them. It can take a discussion in a new and generative direction that benefits everyone, a new option than never existed before, co-created commitments.

2. **Speak 'my language' with authenticity**

    People buy from people they like. We generally like people whom we trust and respect, who are transparent, honest and can help us along our path to greatness and success. If you choose to speak in an inauthentic manner, they will know, and I assure you no one likes to be 'mirrored and matched' (this is an NLP term for copy and play back someone's language pattern in your communication with them, be it visual, verbal or kinaesthetic). Most of your clients and staff will know what you are trying to do and it will feel like manipulation. Avoid manipulating people, it will never end well.

The voice we often use in our life, be it the voice of the aggressor, the people pleaser, the loner etc. is not our authentic voice. It is simply the voice which has had the most conditioning in our life, it's been compounded through repetition and has become our instant and automatic voice. In order to find your authentic voice you must first update your perception of yourself, by letting go of the limiting beliefs associated with the compounded voice and mask that you wear. For years I had the voice of the people pleaser, never saying how I really felt about something without coming across as antagonising. I have over the years let go of some of my limiting beliefs and uncovered my authentic voice and can say what I need to say in both an assertive and compassionate way.

To find your authentic voice and learn to use that voice and speak your truth with compassion can be worked on with the help of a good coach who has a specialisation in this field. Most MDs and business leaders I speak to generally have a similar response to hiring a coach; if a coach has not done the exact same role as they are doing, then they think that the coach will not be of value. This belief is simply not true.

There is a difference between a mentor, a coach and a sponsor and having someone to fulfil each of these roles in your career is important. A mentor is someone whose work and acumen for business we respect and can learn from. A mentor is someone who has done a role you are doing or want to do, but for longer, and has a wealth of experience to share of how not to do something, so you can carve your own path of how to do things your own way.

A coach is someone who explores with you your deep-rooted beliefs about who you are and who it is that your future self wants you to become. It is our limiting beliefs, inability to see new perspectives and our fear that keep us stuck in our lives. We cling so desperately to the notion that we have always done it this way, which increases the fear of real change. Any change has to begin with you. The role of the coach is to help you at a deeper level, where the change needs to happen, that is not superficial or short lived. This allows the emergence of something new that changes you forever giving your life a new map and a new quality of feeling.

A sponsor is someone who is typically your biggest fan, who is rooting for your success. The person I like to call your cheerleader. It can be anyone, your sponsor does not necessarily need to be from within the workplace. This person always wants what is best for you and really wants nothing more than to see you succeed. In my life I am fortunate enough to have a few sponsors, especially my family who cheer really loudly at each of my wins and pick me up each time I stumble. Choose someone who authentically shows their support and celebrates your victory, without malice and jealousy. Unfortunately our life does not come with a road map and neither does being a leader. All good leaders need support and help with direction. The most successful people surround themselves with people who fulfil each of these roles, to help them succeed and be their best self.

A business is more than the numbers you report each year, it is more than its share price. People make a business and it is the people that have the power to make the business a success, and it is the same people who also have the power to cause it to stumble. Good business leaders plan for this and navigate their ship through stormy waters and come out the other side, a little drenched perhaps as there may have been some casualties along the way. There will also be the survivors who got through the storm with the captain who knows how to steer his/her crew to a better place.

Malaysian Airlines was not that long ago a jewel in the crown of South East Asian air travel, it was an award-winning airline. Great customer service was their priority. After the awful atrocities with their planes and crew going missing, being shot down and crashing, they lost even more money than they had done when low-cost airlines began to take the majority of their short-haul routes. As a business they had to tighten the purse strings. This led to a reduced crew with fewer perks, which in turn had a huge impact on morale, staff were exhausted and they had just seen some of their colleagues lose their jobs.

The airline competition is high; the younger and fresher Middle Eastern airlines with their injection of funding are now winning the awards that were once won by Malaysian Airlines. The thing that has done the most damage is not that they had to make cuts, it was that the previous Malaysian Airlines bosses had not managed change well, which had a direct impact on staff morale. With the low morale, customer service levels have also taken a knock. The repercussion of low customer service on an already strained reputation is fewer people spending money to fly with Malaysian Airlines when there are so many other options. If someone has chosen to fly with you despite all the tragic accidents, make customer satisfaction a priority, no one should have to put up with poor customer service.

A business lags or never gets over its hurdles for a number of reasons. The most common are:

- **P**oor leadership

- **L**ack of skills

- **U**nwilling to change, always doing what they have always done

- **O**perating from a place of fear

Poor leadership can be the end of an organisation. Poor leaders often lack self-awareness of how they come across to other people, or are simply disengaged from their business. The hurdles they have faced along the way have left them detached and demotivated from the reason they started the business in the first place. If your motivation for starting the business was purely for financial gain, there is nothing wrong with that. It won't, however, help you grow. What is your mission and vision and does it need to be revisited? Why is your organisation the best at what you do in the way that you do it?

Often leaders stumble when they make a poor decision, and unless there is a strong sense of resilience that can get them back to equilibrium, they often make more poor decisions. Be it strategic, HR, recruitment, financial, the list goes on. Pride has already taken a knock and at this point probably cannot handle much more. So asking for help or getting feedback from other people involved is seen as a sign of weakness instead of what it really is: strength. It takes a lot of strength in showing vulnerability. It takes a great deal of resilience to be comfortable with vulnerability. When you spend so much of your life putting up walls, taking on a persona you think you ought to portray, it can be a struggle to show any vulnerability and ask for help. The truth is that if you have a strong senior team they can often nudge you in the right direction. The most successful teams have complementary skills. If your senior team lack certain skills, then you must either look externally to hire for those skills or invest in ongoing training to build the necessary skills. Like a sommelier, you need to find the best pairing for the task at hand.

You are used to doing things a certain way. After all, it's worked so far, you have a business that is making money. You are surviving in an uncertain economic climate. Congratulations, that is actually better than other businesses have done. Most businesses don't make it past their first 12 months. If you are a business leader with ambition and a desire to grow, you have the opportunity to challenge yourself and your company to be exceptional. You can do this with the one thing that connects each and every one of us: our humanity.

Leadership teams of thriving businesses have a real desire to grow and better themselves alongside the business. It is as important to do the SWOT (strengths, weaknesses, opportunities and threats) analysis to your business as a whole, as it is to apply this same model to one's staff/team. These organisations know how to leverage the strength and skills of their staff and look to minimise the threats. When a company is thriving it is making money, developing careers and people, compassionately. Leaders of this kind of business know each individual's goals, ambitions, wants, desires, needs, regardless of who the individual is – client or employee. They really bring each person on a journey to helping achieve those individual goals as well as the collective goal. The focus is not solely on what I want or what I can get from you, instead the focus is on what can *we* do *for* and *with* each other?

A great business leader, like a captain of a ship, knows where they are heading and will alter course if and when necessary. It might take you longer to get to your destination but you manage to avoid major disasters. A great leader has a clear plan of action that is communicated to everyone that is sailing the journey with them. Being a good captain means that you need to trust your crew and they need to trust you. I would never go sailing with someone I did not have full faith in. It is not only your knowledge, skills, experience and the money you've invested into the business that will bring you success, it is also your ability to communicate compassionately.

- How do you communicate your values to your teams?

  _____

  _____

  _____

- What principles as an organisation will you not be willing to compromise?

  _____

  _____

- What can you do to create a sense of camaraderie between your employees and teams?

  _____

  _____

  _____

- What have you put in place to help staff keep each other accountable and motivated?

  _____

  _____

  _____

- Where and how can you encourage more creativity and collaboration?

  _____

  _____

  _____

- How do you get more input and feedback from your employees?

  _____

  _____

  _____

- Have you got the right leadership team in place to make up for the skills you are missing?

  _____

  _____

- How are you communicating changes to your team?

  _____

  _____

- Who is your coach?

  _____

    - How many times a year are you committing to working with them?

- Who is your mentor?

  _____

    - How many times a year will you schedule to check in with them?

- Who is/are your sponsors?

  _____

    - How many times a month will you connect with them?

Chapter 7:
Empowered teams create

Picture for a minute that you are standing in a shower and there is a bar of wet soap in your hand, and you don't want to drop the soap. You have to use just the right amount of pressure to keep hold of it. If you squeeze too tightly or hold it too lightly it will slip out of your hand and land on the floor and it will be like a game of ice hockey trying to pick it up again. Now imagine that your business is like the bar of soap. If you hold too tightly or don't engage enough there are repercussions.

As a leader there has to be a balance between the two extremes of:

1. holding tightly

2. letting go

When you as a leader disengage from your business, it leaves it directionless and leaderless. If you have no choice but to distance yourself from your business for some time, ensure that the second in command is up to the job, engaged and injects people with confidence.

Joseph is an MD of a tech outsourced agency that was doing well. The company grew and even made a significant profit during the recession, which lasted from 2010 till 2012. This was not the experience held by any of his competitors. There was a real sense of accomplishment, he and his team had got through the thick of it unscathed and client spend was getting bigger. His ambitions were to grow his business and make his mark. He set his sights on the Pan-Asian market; this new adventure took his attention away from his core business in Europe, which since starting his business he was very engaged in and passionate about.

This Pan-Asian adventure had distracted Joseph for three years. During this time, his once thriving business had begun to suffer. Staff motivation and engagement had steadily declined. Joseph would only step in occasionally and became more and more detached. His detachment and frustration would show in his short temper when dealing with issues with his team in Europe. The person Joseph had left second in command, Jamie, was not up to the job. Joseph was not willing to see that he didn't have the right person for the job, even when there was a mass exodus of staff. Joseph's competitors took advantage of his absence and poached a significant number of his staff who were looking for stability and direction. Joseph was just too busy pursuing his next big dream.

The situation was made trickier as Jamie was not very well respected by the staff. He was also notorious for showing favouritism with certain members of staff and it was rumoured that he had made inappropriate advances on some of the female members of the team. Jamie also wasn't seen as someone who was passionate or particularly knowledgeable about the business. He would very often take extended lunch breaks, leave early and was often unreachable when there was an issue. Things were starting to fall apart at the seams.

Joseph had fulfilled his dream of setting up the offices he wanted and on paper at least had grown his business in the Pan-Asian region. He was back, physically at least, and now had to face the music and reality of what had happened over the last few years. His first reaction was annoyance, and he pointed the finger at staff and told them they needed to get their motivation back. Self-motivation is vital in any business and your teams need to be able to bring their motivation to work daily. However, motivation is a complex subject and within a business it is a two-way street. You need to meet your team halfway when it comes to keeping long-term motivation and engagement. People lose motivation when they feel undervalued, taken advantage of, or when they feel treated unjustly. Over the years, Joseph had disengaged and he had alienated some of his key members of staff. Leaving Jamie in charge had not done anything to help those relationships.

> *During a meeting with Joseph, I shared my observations with him: he had lost his passion for his business and to get things back on track he would need to re-engage. I also brought his awareness to the fact that it was his distractions and absence (mentally and emotionally) that had the biggest impact, and he would need to either invest in training for Jamie or find a replacement for that position, as Jamie did nothing to ease the stress everyone felt being left leaderless. Jamie's behaviour and attitude were not in keeping with the values and principles that the employees were used to, those held by the company from the start, the values which once made them a great organisation that managed to weather the hardest storms.*

On the flip side there are those business owners/leaders that unknowingly suffocate their business. Suffocating your staff and controlling every aspect of your business may make you money in the short term, but this type of behaviour is disempowering and verges on bullying. If you have a growth hurdle you want to get over, you have to empower your team and aid creativity. Empowering your teams and creating accountability gives people a sense of ownership and commitment.

I once worked with a brilliant business manager, Alistair. Alistair is an intelligent man and very likeable. We had worked together on a large client pitch. He was very collaborative and really involved his clients and team in decisions. He would never make assumptions about what people would and would not be able to do, unless the client had specifically asked him to make an assumption. He showed the importance of preparation, yet the preparation needed to allow space for decisions to be made by the client and the whole team. From that first meeting Alistair and I had gone to together and each subsequent meeting, we never failed to win new business. You can just breathe a little and let things happen organically.

Just remember your clients are people too and want to be heard and have their input taken into account. Clients do still want to see what is possible; they also want to be part of deciding what is right for them. You will never know the client's business as well as your client, so do not assume to, it will only alienate them. Do not pre-decide for people what you will do and make any assumptions unless they have specifically asked you to. The process of working with clients well is collaboration and co-creation. Empower your team and they will create great solutions with your clients.

There are organisations where, like big brother, they actively watch each computer stroke the employees make and this kills creativity through a culture of fear. At one such organisation the operations director would remotely and secretly log in to people's machines while they were working and just watch what they were doing. The employees were treated like they were at a nursery. There was a huge lack of trust, with staff not being allowed to manage their own time. The staff were trusted so little that they had to use the organisation's own approved Skype account, and every conversation was recorded. What baffled me even more were what to me seemed like insane processes of keeping tabs on people. There was a shared Outlook calendar, where each person had to fill in details of all their meetings, hospital appointments and holidays, so that anyone, at any time, could check where someone was. This is a great system when you have 10 or 15 employees, but when there are 70 it is a messy bureaucratic process. I would assume that it would be enough for someone's line manager to know where they were at any given time during the work day.

Andrea set up her business in her early 30s, having seen how much money she was making her employers, she decided she was going to do this for herself. There were very few senior female business leaders and CEOs at that time and she had hit a glass ceiling. She took some of her clients and colleagues with her and set up on her own.

Andrea started her business at a time when it was still tough for a successful woman in a very male-dominated world. Like a lot of women I know, Andrea put the softness and vulnerability of her femininity aside, in favour of what was seen as the alpha male traits of being tough, controlling and basically 'a bit of a prick'. She had done very well over the years, made a lot of money and had some great client logos to boast about. Over the years her business grew from 5 employees to 70 yet she still relinquishes control of nothing. She gets involved in every account plan and wouldn't think twice in publicly humiliating her staff. She criticised her account management team for putting in their own observations and perspectives on the account plans, even though it was the account team who managed the day-to-day client relationship. Andrea always felt she was right and that her word was final, even if it was incorrect.

As an organisation you will do well in being open to letting data and facts trump any decision made by the highest paid person in the room. It is your day-to-day account team who work with your clients on a regular basis and collect the feedback necessary to populate account plans, so that they can work out exactly how to improve the offering and service to the client. As a business leader, it is vital to listen to what the team have to say and if you do not agree with what they are saying, then have a discussion. If anyone contradicted her she would be sarcastic and humiliate that person, to make an example of them. Andrea's staff would do exactly as she said from a fear of being the next victim of her scorn.

Give your staff the space to breathe and make decisions; if they simply do what you say, they may not be serving your client in the best way. By all means have your team check in with you – after all, you have a wealth of knowledge and experience that can help them – but resist the temptation to take control of everything. Be the person that the team respect, not fear; the person that they will go to for help and advice, not the person who they are too scared to approach when they need support, it will only lead to them making mistakes. When they make mistakes, if you lose your cool it is like taking a pitchfork to your employees' confidence; the more you chip away at their confidence, the more mistakes they are likely to make. It becomes a vicious cycle. Staff begin to act from a place of fear and creativity is squashed by stress.

The next generation of female leaders have the luxury of embracing more of their feminine power and bringing it to the fore. Women who set up businesses in the 20th century, similar to Andrea, had to shout to be heard, who as women felt they had to reject the 'softer' feminine qualities of communication, love, compassion, kindness, vulnerability etc. These softer qualities were seen as a weakness and thus these women drove all their energy into their ferocity, in striving to be taken seriously and get a seat at the predominantly alpha male table.

It is only now that women have begun to embrace these softer feminine qualities within business. What was once seen as vulnerability is in fact a strength and bringing these qualities into your interactions helps you see different perspectives. Regardless of your gender, compassion is a key ingredient in creating an incredible business. There is an added strength in embracing the feminine qualities of gentleness and kindness, while being business savvy and with the masculine and a tiny pinch of alpha male thrown in for good measure in the form of confidence. I know this is a feeling I share with many men and women of my generation that I speak to who are now setting up their own businesses. The world needs more compassion and kindness and less greed, power and control that created most of our mess to begin with, enabling us to move towards a business model of conscious capitalism, caring for the wider society we are all part of, and making money.

The great thing about empowering your teams is that it allows people to shine, collaborate and share knowledge without the need of your constant input. It frees you up to pursue productive endeavours. When business leaders hoard their knowledge they are usually operating from a place of fear – fear of the loss of their power over another. When you give away your knowledge, sharing what you know, it helps your team make better decisions and is ultimately in the best interest of your business. You cannot teach wisdom, wisdom comes with experience. You can certainly guide people in the right direction. Great business leaders bring people along for the journey towards success by making them successful too, even empowering individuals to surpass their own success by arming them with the knowledge they could have done with early on in their career.

"Knowledge is knowing that a tomato is a fruit; wisdom is knowing not to put it in a fruit salad."

Anonymous

You have to let your teams find wisdom by themselves and this comes with experience. By all means, if they are going to crash and burn, step in. The best thing to do is to create such a relationship that they feel confident enough to come and ask you to share your wisdom before they get into a pickle.

Giving your team the power to be collaborative and share knowledge creates a culture of curiosity and desire to create. This culture of curiosity gives people the freedom to ask questions and challenge one another. They will then, without any input from you, come up with a new way and the business will evolve like a living ecosystem that is self-sustaining and that adapts as needed. It brings in a sense of play, the team become the game changers of your industry and are happy to break the mould and be the best as a collective. It is what will bring you more business and create new sources of income. Think of all the new possibilities you could be helping to create just by giving people the freedom to create.

When your team collaborate with your clients, they can create new ways of working together that even you could not predict. It helps create a great balanced client relationship where expectations can be managed and becomes more of a partnership. If you and your staff have a habit of asking "how high?" each time a client tells you to jump, then changing the way you work with these particular clients will take significant effort, patience and perseverance. Any changes that you introduce to this existing client will likely be faced with resistance because you have already set expectations that you will do anything they say and never question or challenge them. I suggest that if you are going to work in a truly collaborative way with a client, and it's all new to you, start as you mean to go on, in a way that is sustainable and gives you and your team space to be creative.

Early in my career one of the largest accounts I managed was a large American computer manufacturer. My then MD left her account management team with a fairly free rein on how we managed our clients. We would create e-books for clients that would be used in email campaigns. The email campaign along with the e-book for this client did not produce the results they were hoping for. Subsequently I had gone to meet my client and sat around the dining table in her house and together we worked out a way we could re-use the asset she had developed with us in several other ways internally at her organisation. This did not necessarily generate immediate income for me, but what it did do was to allow my client to be successful, and over the course of several years she happily sent me through referrals. I was empowered by my business leaders to help create something new with my client, and in turn the relationship that this empowerment allowed me to build brought in one of our highest paying clients of the next two years.

Once you empower your teams, they will be working for you from a place of commitment and loyalty instead of fear. Do you really want people working for you because they feel they have to? When there are people working on my team, I want them to be there because they want to be and are happy working with me. You want to have people on your side that want to be successful and help hit the targets we are set, as well as reaching their own goals. I am sure you want the type of people on your team that when anything goes wrong will not pass the buck but who will all collectively work on a solution. When your staff are empowered, they take responsibility and pride in their work. However, there are always exceptions to the rule.

I had a discussion about my book and my research with some really good friends of mine from university; they are both doing very well and are both in leadership roles for very successful international businesses. One is the VP of a food and beverage organisation and the other is the CEO of a consulting company. We were talking about the concept of people's roles being a privilege and not a right and the need for compassion in business. They had pointed out something that I already knew: a lot of people in business, possibly even you, feel a sense of entitlement to your position: *I worked hard for it, I went to business school and earned my MBA, I took the risk of setting up this business in a hard economic time, I invested my time and money, I worked my way up, etc.* I am guessing the monologue we each play in our heads is more or less similar to this. It is important to acknowledge your achievements. Think of all the opportunities that you have been given or created and made the most of in your life to get you to the position you are now in. You have worked hard and do deserve wonderful things in your life. You are also in a position where you have a responsibility to the people who work for you. I am not talking about a superficial exchange of money for time they spend doing a mundane task for you. You are in the fortunate position that you can help your employees change their life and become successful. Your position allows you the opportunity to expand your own learning and world view by stretching your empathy muscle.

Google is an example of an employer that empowers its teams to create. Yes, this is self-serving to Google, as it does make a significant amount of money from empowering its people. At the same time, it gives people the opportunity to create things they would never have been able to do alone and without the data and technology at their disposal at Google. Like a self-driving car and contact lenses that can measure the blood sugar levels specifically for signalling to diabetics when they need to take their medication. Who says that making money is a bad thing? You are in business to make money. I am not suggesting that you become a philanthropist and give away all your wealth and end up having to rent out your home. What I am suggesting is, as a business owner or leader, perhaps shift your perspective of your position from one of entitlement to one of the position you are in is a privilege. This shift has to happen if we are to in any way become part of the future we need to create.

We can initiate change on a macro level by starting with a change in the micro level. By focusing on what you can do within your own organisation to empower in a way that is mutually beneficial and compassionate is a good start. A single drop of water can create a ripple across an entire lake. Who is to say that a change in your organisation wouldn't help change other companies within your industry and eventually out into the world? We have to begin creating a way of working and communicating with one another that is sustainable. As a business leader, do not be too proud to go to the kitchen every so often to make your team a round of tea/coffee. Be human, bring more of your humanity into your organisation and help your team feel empowered to be the best at what they do.

There was a woman on my team, Rebecca, whose fiancé also worked in the same organisation. They had both started at the organisation in the exact same job role weeks apart and worked on the same account. One worked with the clients based in APAC and the other worked with the clients at the same account based in EMEA. The CEO had taken a real shine to Rebecca's fiancé and had given him opportunities and, uncharacteristically for this CEO, had shared her knowledge with him. She had empowered him to make decisions without having to consult her. Unsurprisingly, Rebecca's fiancé had been promoted several times and now earned significantly more than she did. Her confidence had taken a hit and she was fearful of the CEO, who treated her with disdain and was particularly impatient with her. The attention the EMEA clients received had suffered as a result of Rebecca's inability to make decisions from her lack of confidence. Had Rebecca been given the same opportunities to shine and be empowered as her fiancé had been, the CEO would have been able to see for herself what Rebecca's true potential to shine actually was.

You do not have to be friends with the people who work for you. If you learn how to communicate with compassion and empower people, it will bring out the best in them and help you be more successful. Part of empowering your team to be the best they can be is to provide them with the right tools and knowledge to create new opportunities. Always be clear in your communication to your team of your expectations, set boundaries and let them know who they can go to for help if they need it. Then step away and don't interfere with the process of them doing the job you hired them for. Those that are great will shine through. Give everyone the same chance to succeed.

"An investment in knowledge always pays the best interest."

Benjamin Franklin

- How are you going to share your knowledge?

  _____

  _____

  _____

- How will you encourage collaboration and co-creation?

  _____

  _____

  _____

- What training does your team need?

  _____

  _____

  _____

- What opportunities have you given one specific person and not another? How will you remedy this?

  _____

  _____

  _____

- What opportunities can you create for growth and development?

  _____

  _____

  _____

  _____

- How can you give your team more freedom?

  _____

  _____

  _____

- How will you choose to react if things don't go as planned?

  _____

  _____

  _____

- Who will you work with to help create a solution?

  _____

  _____

  _____

Chapter 8:
It takes a tribe to raise a child

Our responsibility does not end at ourselves, partners, family, friends or businesses. We have a responsibility to the wider community and a wider global responsibility. We each have a responsibility to look after our planet, to the oneness of humanity and showing our compassion to our fellow human and all living beings. Many of us choose to not see it as a responsibility at all because we are sitting in our own bubbles of existence. It is easier to simply ignore the issues as '*it's got nothing to do with me*' or '*let the government worry about it*'. We cannot be so ignorant as to believe that simply ignoring the problems we face in the world will make them go away and they are someone else's problem. They are everyone's problem. If we continue our selfish pursuit of wealth with no regard to the cost, there will be a higher price to pay later on. It will be your debt to humanity and we become nothing more than monsters. It is this very greed-driven behaviour which created the problems in the first place.

There is a systemic and sustainable approach to solving the issues we face in our world. The solution to the problem is not some place 'out there', it is right here, exactly where you are – in your home, your business, your immediate environment – the small daily changes you can implement to be part of a wider solution. We often see the wider world problems as not having an impact on us.

An example of how we make problems worse in our pursuit of wealth is the impact that our demand/need for cheaply produced foods has on the planet. Cheaply produced foods often contain palm oil. In order for palm oil to be produced, land needs to be cleared and it is rainforest that is usually cleared to make room for new palm oil estates to pop up. We are shown the images of burning and dying orangutans on television charity adverts in a quest to help save them. The burning of rain forests doesn't only cause devastation to the orangutans and the entire rainforest ecosystem, it causes a great deal of suffering to human life as well. Poorly managed toxic waste from these palm oil plantations pollutes our seas, the fish we consume and creates haze over our cities. The rainforest in Indonesia has been burned to the ground to make way for palm oil estates and is having a massive impact on the environment. The most obvious is the toxic haze that has enveloped Malaysia, Singapore and Indonesia over the last decade and has reached toxic levels. According to Professor Roy Harrison, a professor of environmental health at the University of Birmingham, "*The particles in the air are mostly made up of carbon compounds and sooty material and there will be nasty acrid gases in the smoke.*"

The reported effects of the haze included problems with breathing, wheezing, coughing and watery eyes. In the long term, prolonged exposure to air pollution of any kind can have an impact on human health and reduce life expectancy. Air pollution kills around 7 million people every year according to the World Health Organization (WHO), accounting for one in eight deaths worldwide in 2012. The main causes of death were stroke and heart disease, followed by chronic obstructive pulmonary disease (COPD), lung cancer, and respiratory infections among children. There are certain groups who are particularly at risk: elderly people and those with respiratory illnesses, such as asthma, are vulnerable when haze hits because their lungs are less able to deal with the pollution. They are more likely to be admitted to hospital and the haze becomes an additional stress factor. People with asthma find their condition worsens and they need to take more medication. Children are thought to be susceptible to the dangers of air pollution because they spend more time outdoors and breathe in more air per unit of body weight. Professor Harrison says that younger adults can also be affected. A new study by WHO predicts that by 2050 air pollution could be the cause of 6.6 million premature deaths every year worldwide.

Recent research led by Dr Krishnan Bhaskaran, a statistical epidemiologist from the London School of Hygiene and Tropical Medicine, discovered that high pollution events could trigger heart attacks in people who were already vulnerable. *"We do know that exposure to particles in air pollution affects the rhythm of the heart. This could affect people in their forties who are beginning to have heart conditions which they may not be aware of."*

If we don't even care about humanity, what chance has Mother Earth or any animal got to have our attention and action? So make humanity a priority over profits, so we can begin to solve the wider world problems together as a collective. We can then focus our attention and energy on making the necessary changes to help the planet and create sustainable solutions for our needs and wants, as a collective.

Problems tend to be viewed as belonging to an individual, and it is seen as that individual's sole responsibility to find a solution. The problems of the people around you, whether you wish to admit it or not, will impact you in some way, shape or form. If addressing haze and rainforest issues in South East Asia is too far from your reality, then let's look at this from the perspective of your business. If your employees are having personal problems or work problems, it will impact concentration, attention, creativity and productivity. Their problems then become your problem too, because it has impacted your business. The usual reaction to this is for business leaders to get annoyed. After you pay them, they should get their head in the game. There is a real sense of isolating the individual and his/her problem, with no willingness to help, "*I don't know what's going on with you outside of work but that's your problem. I expect you to bring your 'A' game to work*". There are organisations that do hire business coaches and therapists to help their staff, which is a wonderful way of helping other people while helping you. It shows compassion and caring, and is a way of accepting that you too have a responsibility to that person as a human.

A very close friend of mine spent many years travelling through Africa and told me a detailed story of a tribe who would solve their problems as a collective. While she was staying in this village as a volunteer nurse, there was a couple who were having marital issues. The elders of the tribe had made arrangements for the couple and the entire village to meet in a sacred space. The couple were told to sit opposite each other in the centre of the circle. They were soon joined by everyone else from the village, including their respective families, neighbours and friends, who made a large circle around them.

The village elder spoke first, in a native language my friend did not understand, but her translator did the best they could to help fill her in on what was going on. It seemed that the village elder was setting the scene and letting everyone know that the couple were having some troubles. He had invited the couple to each take turns to speak and voice what the problems were from their own perspective. Each had to stay silent while the other spoke. Everyone then gave their opinion on how the couple could solve their problems. Once everyone had a chance to speak, the couple and each person present would each be held accountable for doing their part in helping to fix the problem. A neighbour said he would not keep the husband out for so long at night talking to him so the young man could go home to his hut and help his wife with their new baby, and be there with her. So on and so forth. Each person that offered a solution to the couple's problems took responsibility for helping solve the problem. I am certain it is the root of the saying 'it takes a tribe to raise a child' and in this instance it took a tribe to keep a young family together.

I was told that the tribe's men and women played very traditional roles. The men of the village go out to hunt, and the women look after the village and homes. Each person has something they can contribute and each person is happy to be accountable for what they have committed to doing, be it to teach the husband to be a better hunter, or to teach the wife to dry meat instead of salting it. Everyone is accountable, and everyone sharing in solving the problems, they do not point blame or shame, they simply work out a solution together. Not blaming and shaming builds trust. If you alienate or humiliate someone you lose their trust and it damages your relationship. It is important to be persistent and consistent. Anyone who has built a business or raised children knows that you need to put in effort, love and care to both of them to get the results you want. Nothing and no one is perfect, a lot of life is trial and error. Once you learn from the errors, move on. By creating a supportive environment around you and each of your staff, be aware that while I think open door policies are great and I am all for them, keep scheduled time sacred.

The more hierarchical an organisation, the more issues there tend to be with communication and respect. Hierarchical organisation structures are regimented as to who each person can go to for support. If someone does not get on with their line manager, there has to be another way of helping them deal with their problems, rather than forcing them to talk to someone they just do not get on with. Messages tend to filter through the chain of command and get changed along the way to suit each person's agenda. Help create the supportive environment to help people overcome hurdles and better them, get a coach and a mentor. Expect that there will be some resistance to change, remember to keep the momentum and commitment to changing and creating an environment that encourages communication and collaboration.

Building a business is like raising a child; no matter what you have planned, there is almost always something that will not go as planned and you need to wing it. Get the support you need as a business leader to be the best you can be, for your business to flourish. Get a coach and don't be too proud to ask for help or advice; we are all social animals, you do not have to be alone in trying to fix things by yourself. Realign your social construct to allow for things to come together in a way to offer you support. You often need support in dealing with difficult situations and working through your own resistance and the things you may overreact to. There are so many times that you might need directions to tap into your infinite internal resources so that you can face and overcome the beliefs that currently hold you back and find solutions to hurdles that stop you from creating a compassionate working environment that will help you generate a successful thriving business. As a business leader, it is vital that you build up, keep your confidence levels up and look to expand your paradigms. Allow the paradigm shifts to happen, it can be as simple an exercise as walking in someone else's shoes, to be able to identify the difference between one's territory and map, i.e. the difference between fact and opinion/personal experience.

Your employees are the people who support you, and if you support them in their development and growth, together you make your business successful. They are the ones helping you raise this 'child' (your business). Keep their skills topped up by giving them the best training you can afford to build up their skills so they too can be great. If and when they leave your business, be it to join another one or start their own, be proud in the knowledge that you helped them succeed in their life. If they stay, well that's great for you, because you know you have the best person at that job working with you.

Many business leaders I speak to who want to run culture change/transformation initiatives don't really know the areas that need improvement. As a business leader, knowing and understanding your company culture is important when mapping out the changes you wish to see. This process can be particularly hard for a business leader who takes negative feedback, from the internal and external surveys, personally. Feedback allows you to build a picture of what the current state of affairs is from many different perspectives. It is an opportunity to learn and work out what exactly needs development and planning. The plans are the maps to get you from where you are now to where you want to be as an organisation.

Would you be happy for your children or someone else you really care about to work in your business as an employee at a junior level? If the answer is no, then the questions you need to ask yourself are:

- What kind of culture and environment do I want to create?

- What can I improve on?

- When will I make these improvements by?

- How will I do this?

- What does the action plan look like?

- Who else needs to be involved in facilitating these changes?

- How can I hold my team accountable for the changes?

- What will be the measure of success?

Drive and commit the time. Many times I have worked in an organisation where people have the best intentions for a specific project in the beginning, enthusiasm is high, people are totally on board with all the great new concepts, but then things get dumped by the wayside. Everyone has to be accountable and you need to help keep the momentum and dialogue going. It is vital that you do not underestimate the value of team building. Your senior team and each senior person with their own teams need to be on the same page.

The culture of division, of 'us and them', has to come to an end. I have worked in the corporate sector long enough to know that sales, marketing, operations, tech, finance and production have always blamed one another for things getting messed up. I am also not naïve enough to think we can all live in a rosy bubble of love, peace and harmony in the workplace. There are personality types in each of those departments which will never really get on. What I do truly believe is that we can all learn to communicate with compassion to reduce the stress we all feel on a daily basis. As a business leader, it is this time that you use wisely to get people all on the same page and communicate to everyone what is going on.

One of the MDs of an organisation I worked at had a saying which I have adopted: '*Good news fast, bad news faster*'. Being open and honest about the bad news is important so the issues can be fixed as soon as possible. It is vital that when someone in your team shares this bad news with you that you react in the best possible way to the bad news. As a business leader, your focus needs to stay with the information you have been given with a mindset of 'what needs to be/can be/will be done to fix the problem?' Once the issue has been dealt with, then begin to address the root cause of why the issue occurred in the first place by having a discussion with everyone involved. Be collaborative to find a solution and just as collaborative in fixing the root cause of the issues. Encourage people to share news that is not so good ASAP before it becomes an issue. Your reaction to information will have a significant impact on how comfortable your employees are with passing information to you and the anxiety levels that build up around a specific situation.

In business always keep in mind that people buy from people, and the investment you make in the people that work for you through empowerment, encouragement, training, respect, trust and compassion will give you incredible results.

I was invited to attend a client meeting in New York by a large global technology vendor. It was a strategic planning meeting on how to help this large globally recognised brand to improve their revenue. It was a week of meetings where, as you can imagine, schedules were fairly packed and we worked long hours. There were several attendees at one meeting which represented different businesses and areas of expertise; some attendees were there to play a part as potential suppliers in the delivery of the objectives of this large organisation. There were representatives of six external businesses at this meeting (of which I was one), all of whom, apart from me, was from the US, so perhaps my assumption was that they would know more about the culture and how best to 'behave' in this cultural setting. I thought I would follow their lead, I am I glad I stuck to my instincts and chose to do things the way I knew to be right.

Four of the other agency representatives felt that it was appropriate to deliver a hard pitch during a strategy meeting. I thought well maybe this is the American way of participating in a strategy meeting, or simply that the other four company representatives were just inexperienced in 'reading a room'. I can tell you that after that meeting the only two companies that this organisation didn't fire was the one I represented and another organisation whose business owner was wise enough to know that this meeting was all about focusing on solving the issues the client faced.

Unless business is about setting up a one-off pop-up stall selling fish in a market, then the behaviour exhibited by the other four agencies is inappropriate. If you had sent one of your employees to a meeting like this and they represented you in this way, then I am certain you would have been sorely disappointed on losing such a valuable deal. The skills and level of investment you need to make into your employees' success cannot be underestimated. If one of your team is meeting with a very senior leadership team with representatives from across the globe, they need to behave like a consultant, be professional and respectful to all parties in the room.

Great opportunities like this do not come knocking every day and when they are wasted because people do not know how to listen or communicate well it is such a shame. The purpose of the meeting was to focus on the issues the clients had and as part of this we each had to give a bit of an overview of the organisation we each represented, as an introduction to everyone in the room and our area of expertise, to be of help. The people that were pitching (who got the boot) unfortunately had the stereotypical 'hot shot', 'think I'm all that' type of personality, with very little in the form of humility or empathy for the client's problem. They were the type of people that give sales professionals a bad name.

I've known some incredible sales people, whom I have worked with or met across several countries in the Americas, Europe, Asia and Africa. The qualities the best sales people have in common are:

- Always focus on the client's objectives and issues, so you can co-create the best solution

- Know when they don't know something – they don't just 'wing it', they bring in the right experts at the right time

- Great listening skills

- Can read people well

- Compassionate – show humanity to everyone and are humble

- Are the trusted adviser – challenge the client when necessary to help them get better results and point them in the right direction even if it means away from you

- Build good relationships – communication and trust are key

- Always close the right deals and get repeat business

- Take feedback and input on how to improve

In this modern world where competition is global, you need to learn all of the above. It might even transform the culture of your organisation to one that cares about the people behind each deal internally and externally. People buy from people, be a person first and the rest will follow.

Invest in people's growth and development and they in turn will invest in you. I have said before that your position in the organisation is a privilege not a right; you have the power to really make a difference and be part of the solution our world so desperately needs. Slavery was abolished many years ago, keeping the mentality and culture of master and slave with your staff not only does damage to them but to you too. Make people feel sad about leaving your organisation and feel like they have learnt a lot and bettered themselves. As a human race we have been striving and working towards justice and fairness for millennia; make this a reality in your organisation by doing the following:

- Listen to what staff have to say and let them know they can come to you with a problem, and if they do come to you with a problem, ask that they try to also come with a potential solution to that problem.

- Schedule in time to discuss the problems and give people your undivided attention.

- Teach people to communicate with compassion, so things do not get personal. The '*you made me do this*', '*you didn't do that*', '*you did this*' type of discussions need to change. People need to take ownership of their reactions and feelings. No one can make you do anything. You are not a puppet, so don't let anyone pull your strings. Your reactions are entirely your own, we all choose how we react to any given stimuli.

Good leaders can only do this when they know themselves. I've said many times already that the three most senior people within an organisation create the culture. You need to lead by example, i.e. '*do as I do*' and not '*do as I say*'. Be aware of yourself first before you plan on attempting to know and influence others. I suggest that you pick one opportunity for improvement and work on that, making a commitment to it. Set yourself a goal to make it happen. If your team see you are working on making changes and improvements to yourself, they will be more inclined to want to do that for themselves.

- How will you create a forum for people to share news?

  _____

  _____

  _____

  _____

- How will you give and receive feedback?

  _____

  _____

  _____

  _____

- What traits does your tribe need in order to raise your business? And how will you encourage or train those traits?

  _____

  _____

  _____

  _____

- What small changes can you implement that can help address wider world issues?

_____

_____

_____

- How can you make your business practices more sustainable?

_____

_____

_____

- What can you do to change what you do as an organisation to have a positive impact on the environment?

_____

_____

_____

  - What can you do to encourage your suppliers to also make a positive contribution to the environment?

_____

_____

_____

Bibliography

Sigmund Freud. *The Ego and the Id*. Hogarth Press 1962

Chade-Meng Tan, Daniel Goleman, Jon Kabat-Zinn. *Search Inside Yourself: The Unexpected Path to Achieving Success, Happiness (and World Peace)*. HarperCollins 2013

Lewis Carroll. *The Complete Works of Lewis Carroll*. Penguin Books Ltd; New edition (17 Oct. 1988)

Geoffrey Zubay. *Biochemistry*, 3rd edition, Wm. C. Brown Publishers 1993

Per Brodal. *The central nervous system: structure and function*. OUP USA; 4th edition (15 April 2010)

Stephen Gillingham & Robert Dilts. *A Hero's Journey*. Crown House Publishing Ltd. 2009

John Hubbard. *The peripheral nervous system*. Springer 2013

Otto Scharmer – Ulab. See: https://www.edx.org/

U.Lab was designed by a Presencing Institute (PI) team, in partnership with MITx. The Presencing Institute, co-founded by Otto Scharmer, is an awareness-based action-research community that creates social technologies, builds capacities, and generates holding spaces for profound social change.

Dalai Lama. Creating a happier world. See: http://www.actionforhappiness.org/dalai-lama-event

Richard Davidson. Creating a happier world. See: http://www.actionforhappiness.org/dalai-lama-event and http://centerhealthyminds.org/about/founder-richard-davidson

Malaysian Airlines. See: http://www.channelnewsasia.com/news/business/new-malaysia-airlines-ceo/1834646.html

Ben & Jerry's. See: http://www.benjerry.co.uk/flavours/chocolate-fudge-brownie-ice-cream

Innocent. See: http://www.innocentdrinks.co.uk/us/our-story

Google. See:

- http://www.businessknowhow.com/internet/googlesp.htm

- http://www.google.co.uk/about/company/facts/culture/

- https://www.ted.com/speakers/dan_cobley

Holmes & Rhae. See:

- https://en.wikipedia.org/wiki/Holmes_and_Rahe_stress_scale

- http://www.simplypsychology.org/SRRS.html

- http://www.stress.org/holmes-rahe-stress-inventory/

World population. See: http://www.theguardian.com/environment/series/crowded-planet-population+world/population

CIPD recruitment survey report. See: http://www.cipd. co.uk/NR/rdonlyres/746F1183-3941-4E6A-9EF6-135C29AE22C9/0/recruitmentsurv07.pdf

The Invention of the Light Bulb: Davy, Swan and Edison see: http://www.enchantedlearning.com/inventors/edison/lightbulb.shtml

O.C. Tanner Study. See: http://blog.octanner.com/wp-content/uploads/sites/3/2013/06/employee-recognition-research-employee-awards-programs-wp.pdf

Rewrap. See: http://www.re-wrap.com/home

Haze in South East Asia. See: http://www.bbc.co.uk/news/health-23000409

http://edition.cnn.com/2015/01/27/asia/asia-air-pollution-haze/

Dan Price. See: http://www.independent.co.uk/news/world/americas/dan-price-ceo-who-increased-minimum-wage-to-70000-is-renting-out-his-home-to-make-ends-meet-10433097.html

http://time.com/money/3831828/ceo-raise-70000-dan-price/

About the Author

Kavitha Chahel MBA FRSA

Kavitha is the founder and MD of a coaching and training business Compassionism Ltd, focusing on developing compassionate leaders, to create effective teams and happy humans.

She is an experienced business coach and company director. For nearly 20 years Kavitha has worked in business development, marketing, business leadership and strategy across the corporate, public and charitable sectors. Kavitha is also a non-executive director of Asha projects, a charity that provides safe housing to women and children fleeing from domestic violence. She has worked with clients across EMEA, The Americas & APAC.

Kavitha is a speaker and has been a guest lecturer at the University of Middlesex and London Metropolitan University.

She is married to her university sweetheart, they live in the leafy county of Surrey and they have a dog named Oreo.

To learn more about Kavitha, and the services offered by her company Compassionism Ltd please visit www.compassionism.com

Twitter: @compassionism

YouTube: www.youtube.com/compassionismltdkc

19823521R00107

Printed in Great Britain
by Amazon